JOHN COTTON
PATRIARCH OF NEW ENGLAND

A. W. McClure

Edited by Nate Pickowicz

John Cotton: Patriarch of New England

Copyright 2019 by Nate Pickowicz

This work is an abridged, edited, and retitled version of a work in public domain, titled, *The Life of John Cotton* by A. W. McClure, excerpted from the *Lives of the Chief Fathers of New England* series: Volume 1. Boston: Massachusetts Sabbath School Society, Depository, No. 13 Cornhill. 1846.

Cover: Boston Church, Lincolnshire, 1821 James Harrison

All rights reserved. No part of this edition may be reproduced in any form without the written permission from the author.

Published by: H&E Publishing, Peterborough, Canada

First Edition, 2019
Paperback ISBN: 978-1-989174-23-4

About the Editor

Nate Pickowicz is the pastor of Harvest Bible Church in Gilmanton Iron Works, New Hampshire. He is the author of *Reviving New England: The Key to Revitalizing Post-Christian America* and *Why We're Protestant: An Introduction to the Five Solas of the Reformation*. He has edited several books, including John Calvin's *Justification by Faith* for H&E Publishing. He is a Teaching Fellow with Reformanda Ministries, and contributes to *Table Talk* magazine. He and his wife, Jessica, have two children, Jack and Elizabeth.

Contents

Foreword vii
Phil Johnson

Introduction to the New Edition xv
Nate Pickowicz

John Cotton: Patriarch of New England

General Introduction 1

1. Early Life & Education 9

2. Boston, Lincolnshire 19

3. Persecutions & Translation 27

4. Boston, Massachusetts 57

5. Controversies 77

6. Legacy 103

Works Cited 147

The Writings of John Cotton 149

FOREWORD

Phil Johnson

Among the luminaries of the early Puritan era, none shines brighter than John Cotton. He possessed a remarkable array of spiritual gifts and academic accomplishments. He was a brilliant scholar, a master of the biblical languages, a skilled and perceptive theologian, a proficient writer, a powerful preacher, a tenderhearted pastor, a wise and sympathetic counselor, and an effective evangelist. He had lengthy ministries both in England and in colonial Massachusetts. On both sides of the Atlantic he managed to gain profound and lasting respect from friends and adversaries alike. His character and personality shaped the unique flavor of American Puritanism more than any other single influence. The very best qualities we see among the Puritans of early Massachusetts—their humble piety, their emphasis on sin and repentance, their strong work ethic, their sense of duty to God and community, and their love for Christ and Scripture—all are part of John Cotton's legacy.

During the first decade of the seventeenth century, John Cotton was a lecturer and catechist at Emmanuel

College, Cambridge University (a Puritan training institution for pastors). Though he was highly esteemed for his eloquence and erudition, Cotton himself was not yet genuinely converted. A sermon by Richard Sibbes in 1609 truly awakened his heart to believe, and the transformation was immediate and obvious to all. The trademark eloquence of Cotton's lectures gave way to a simple but passionate style of gospel-focused preaching designed not to impress fellow scholars, but rather to awaken the consciences of his hearers. The need for sound conversion is one of the central themes that reverberates through all of Cotton's subsequent sermons and writings.

His fondness for gospel truth was both winsome and infectious. Wherever he preached, people were convicted and converted. A thoroughgoing Calvinist, he powerfully refuted the opinion of those who insist that the doctrine of election is an impediment to evangelism. He was a zealous and effective winner of souls. Just a few months after Cotton's ordination to the ministry in colonial Massachusetts, the First Church of Boston saw a wave of remarkable conversions that can only be termed *revival*. Governor Winthrop wrote,

> It pleased the Lord to give special testimony of his presence in the church of Boston, after Mr. Cotton was called to office there. More were converted and added to that church, than to all the other churches in the bay.... Divers profane and notorious evil persons came and confessed their

sins, and were comfortably received into the bosom of the church.¹

It is of course extraordinary that a renowned theologian, scholar, and long-tenured pastor of John Cotton's stature and age (he was nearly 50) would leave everything he knew in order to help establish a colony in the brutal frontier of the New World. How John Cotton came to Massachusetts is one of the central threads in the story of his remarkable life. You can't read any biographical account of John Cotton without noticing the amazing way Providence sovereignly directed this amazing spiritual leader into a role he would never have chosen for himself—and thus magnified his influence and his legacy through circumstances that would have seemed more likely to sideline him or bury his name in obscurity.

Cotton's legacy lives on. His life is instructive even today.

There are, for example, profound lessons about separatism and schism woven into John Cotton's experience. We learn from his struggle with the Church of England that cautious, biblical separatism (2 Corinthians 6:14–18; Revelation 18:4) is sometimes necessary. On the other

---

[1] James Kendall Hosmer, LL.D., ed. *Winthrop's Journal "History of New England," 1630–1649*, vol. 1 (New York: Charles Scribner's Sons, 1908), 116.

hand, Cotton himself correctly believed that the schismatic mentality of those who think every disagreement and every error deserves a harsh anathema is destructive to the health and testimony of the church. Faithful believers need to foster both wise biblical discernment and a unifying love for the true Bride of Christ.

This is vividly illustrated not only in John Cotton's failed struggle to remain in and influence the Church of England, but also in his well-documented conflicts with Roger Williams. Williams was a strict separatist who refused communion with the Puritan churches of Massachusetts because they declined to condemn the Church of England as a synagogue of Satan. His views about the church, her purity, her unity, and her role in society set Williams bitterly at odds with John Cotton.

Both John Cotton and Roger Williams had valid points to make. For example, Williams alleged that the churches and the government of early Massachusetts afforded hardly more freedom of conscience than the Puritans themselves had been given under Archbishop Laud in England. The complaint was not far-fetched. The churches of New England had no problem letting the secular magistrates inflict punishments on people who were excommunicated over matters of conscience. Virtually all evangelicals today would have more sympathy with Williams's view on that point than with Cotton's.

But Williams was unquestionably too censorious, too sharp in his criticism, too prone to exaggerate others' flaws, too ready to impute ill motives to his adversaries, and too quick to break fellowship with men who gave every evidence of genuine faith in Christ and his Word.

Both men's shortsighted prejudices made their disagreement far more bitter than it needed to be.

One conviction that John Cotton is especially remembered for is his defense of Congregationalism. More than fifteen years before sailing for the New World, he had embraced Congregationalism, a system of church polity where each individual church, rather than the presbytery, is responsible for its own affairs. (New England Congregationalism is another key feature of Cotton's legacy.) In 1644, at the height of his conflict with Roger Williams, Cotton published *The Keyes of the Kingdom of Heaven,* an explanation and defense of Congregationalism. The manuscript was sent by ship to England, where it was published. John Owen, the most eminent of Puritan scholars, obtained a copy in order to write a critique, but upon reading the book, he was converted to John Cotton's point of view. Owen wrote,

> In the pursuit and management of [Mr. Cotton's] work, quite beside, and contrary to my expectation, at a time wherein I could expect nothing on that account but ruin in this world, without the knowledge, or advice of, or conference with any one person of that judgment, I was prevailed upon to receive those principles to which I had thought to have set myself in opposition.

He then wryly added, "Indeed this way of impartially examining all things by the word . . . laying aside all prejudiced respects to persons or present traditions, is a course that I would admonish all to beware of who would avoid the danger of being made [Congregationalists]."[2]

It's a shame John Cotton and Roger Williams didn't take Owen's dispassionate approach to examining one another's views. The two were so different that it's unlikely that either would have fully embraced the other's position, but they certainly could have learned from one another.

That seems an important lesson for Christians living in the polemically charged atmosphere of the Internet age. It's one more thing we need to learn from the life and experience of John Cotton.

The only other significant misstep worth pointing out in the career of John Cotton is his early support for Anne Hutchinson and her followers. In the end, Cotton saw that although she claimed to be echoing his beliefs, she had actually taken aspects of his teaching on grace to an unbiblical, antinomian extreme. He wisely distanced himself from the error and took the opportunity to clarify his views through patient, careful instruction regarding the issues that were under debate.

The deep respect Cotton's contemporaries had for him was well deserved, and he also deserves much credit

---

[2] John Owen, The *Works of John Owen*, vol. 1 (London: Richard Baynes, 1826), 56.

for the moral and biblical foundations that held colonial Massachusetts together from the time of the colony's founding well into the next century. I would argue that the Great Awakening of Jonathan Edwards' era represented a return to New England's spiritual roots—a harvest that sprang from seeds planted by John Cotton and watered by the next two generations of New England Puritans (including Cotton's son-in-law and grandson, Increase Mather and Cotton Mather).

One cannot make sense of early New England history apart from the Puritan influence that shaped that culture—and John Cotton is the key figure in understanding the doctrine, piety, and spirit of New England Puritanism. My hope is that this book will be an introduction for many readers into the rich spiritual history of early New England. May that in turn stir renewed interest in the great biblical truths that shaped the very embryo of American life and values—and (even more foundationally) the lives of the godly men and women who helped found this great nation.

Phil Johnson
Santa Clarita, CA
June 2019

Introduction to the New Edition

Nate Pickowicz

It is nearly impossible to overstate the value of the New England Puritans to the history of American Christianity. While many groups made their way across the Atlantic to the New World, it was the Puritans who first piled up stones in honor of God's faithfulness in bringing them safely to their "City on a Hill." As the church was established in Boston, the Lord provided them with a pastor whose gifts and talents would bless them for decades: the Reverend John Cotton.

Considered to be one of the greatest preachers in his day, Cotton had already established his reputation for Puritan orthodoxy for twenty years at St. Botolph's Church in Boston, Lincolnshire. As one of the last remaining Nonconformist leaders to be chased out of his church by Archbishop Laud, Cotton made his way to a New England that was eagerly waiting for him.

Known as "a devout, grace-oriented man of God,"[1] John Cotton influenced the churches of New England, and pioneered what would come to be known as "The Congregational Way," which would later be adopted by other Puritan ministers such as Thomas Goodwin and John Owen. "No New England minister," writes Beeke and Pederson, "was as influential as Cotton in promoting Congregational church practice."[2]

Beyond his ecclesiological influence, Cotton was a formidable scholar, competent catechist, and dynamic expository preacher. In a day when many towns were struggling to sustain themselves spiritually, the Boston church was experiencing intense revival as hundreds of residents were coming to faith in Jesus Christ through Cotton's labors.

After he died in 1652, John Cotton's ministry still bore fruit. He had spearheaded an effort to draft the Cambridge Platform, which served as the early constitution of Massachusetts. His children's catechism, *Milk for Babes*, became part of *The New England Primer*, which provided theological instruction for nearly every American child for 150 years. Additionally, he published forty works, which were widely read and remained in print for many years.

---

[1] Everett Emerson, *John Cotton*, revised edition (Boston, MA: Twayne, 1990), 4.

[2] Joel R. Beeke and Randall J. Pederson, *Meet the Puritans* (Grand Rapids, MI: Reformation Heritage, 2006), 159.

Introduction to the New Edition

However, early nineteenth-century Unitarianism hijacked Congregationalism from the Puritans, and conveniently discarded the elements they disagreed with, namely, Reformed theology and biblical eldership. Further, their polemical smear campaign effectively swept the entire Puritan movement, including John Cotton, into the dustbin.

While theological liberalism was enjoying its shallow victory however, a small Christian resistance was working to recover the lost memory of the Puritans. A.W. McClure was one of them.

Alexander Wilson McClure

Born in the city of John Cotton on May 8, 1808, Alexander Wilson McClure studied at Yale and Amherst colleges, eventually graduating from Andover Theological Seminary in 1830. Ordained to ministry in the Presbyterian Church, he would pastor the First Congregational Church in Malden, Massachusetts from 1830–1841, and again from 1848–1852. He then moved to New Jersey where he pastored the Dutch Reformed Church in Jersey City from 1852–1855.

In addition to pastoral ministry, Dr. McClure was a revered scholar, a talented dialectician, and a gifted writer. He penned numerous articles for the *Christian Observatory* (of which he served as Editor), *New Brunswick Review*, and the *Literary and Theological Review*. He published several books, including the 2-volume series, *Lives of the Chief Fathers of New England, Lectures on Ultra-Universalism,* and the noteworthy, *The Translators Revived,* which would see 20 editions from 1853 to 2015.

He was known for being a humble and devout minister with a burning heart for the lost. He served as the corresponding secretary for the American and Foreign Christian Union in 1855, and despite failing health, traveled to Rome, Italy in 1856 to serve as a chaplain. Suffering with bronchial disease in 1858, he retired from public service, and died on September 20, 1865 in Canonsburg, Pennsylvania.

The life and works of A.W. McClure are deserving of further treatment elsewhere, but for our purposes, we will briefly look at his biographical work on John Cotton.

The Life of John Cotton (1846)

The recent surge of interest in Puritanism has given us two notable biographies on John Cotton.[3] While a number of early accounts of Cotton's life were written, there were relatively few biographies after 1702.[4] However, in the mid-1800s, Alexander McClure penned a 2-volume biographical series for the Massachusetts Sabbath School So-

---

[3] Larzer Ziff, *The Career of John Cotton: Puritanism and the American Experience* (NJ: Princeton University Press, 1962); and Everett Emerson, *John Cotton.* Revised Edition (Boston, MA: Twayne, 1990).

[4] Cotton Mather, *Magnalia Christi Americana* (London: Thomas Parkhurst, 1702).

ciety recounting the lives of early American Puritan leaders. While the second volume was comprised of short treatments on John Wilson, John Norton, and John Davenport, the first volume, *The Life of John Cotton*, focused exclusively on the eminent Boston divine. Yet these volumes are disregarded by modern scholarship, I believe, for two reasons.

First, these two volumes were written for the purpose of educating general Christian readers. While the prose is by no means simplistic, it lacks the erudition of works written by academians. However, it should be acknowledged that modern popular-level writing is notably simpler than it was two centuries ago, and what was intended for young adults in the 1840s would no doubt carry the interest of twenty-first century readers.

Second, these volumes are unapologetically sympathetic to Christianity. Whereas much of Puritan scholarship today is noticeably secular, dealing with the topic from a strictly historical and psychological perspective, McClure's volumes treat their subjects with love and godly admiration. As a biographer, he is partial not only to the early Puritan founders, but Christianity as a whole. Modern scholarship often scoffs at this approach, treating it as biased, despite the obvious hypocrisy inherent in the fact that many non-Christian historians stand in judgment of Puritanism, stacking it up against their own humanistic worldviews.

While hagiography is largely unhelpful in recounting church history, I believe the best interpreters of Christians of the past are *Christians* of the present. Thankfully, we're starting to see more of this. For example, while secular scholars tend to treat the Puritans' Calvinism as an obtuse anachronism, Christian historians like Iain Murray and Joel Beeke see their understanding of the doctrines of grace as faithful expressions of biblical soteriology. Likewise, McClure operates within this sanctified realm.

The Life of John Cotton is clear, thorough, and beautifully-written. As stated earlier, the work was written for younger readers, but does not insult their intelligence. Building off of the labors of his previous biographers— Samuel Whiting, John Norton, and Cotton Mather— McClure fills out much of the life of John Cotton by placing him in the context of the heels of the English Reformation, and at the birth of New England. While McClure's account has effectively been stricken from the academic record, it serves as a helpful narrative for those discovering John Cotton and American Puritanism for the first time.

A New Edition

For the publication of a new edition, a few editorial changes have been made. First, the manuscript was retyped from the 1846 edition, and includes several modernizations of spelling and format. However, much of the unique phrasing was kept for the purpose of maintaining the original author's voice. Further, section headings

Introduction to the New Edition

have been inserted into the body of the text, and chapter titles have been added.

Additionally, three of the middle chapters on Puritanism and Congregationalism have been removed for the sake of maintaining the narrative flow of the biography. While the information contained is certainly valuable, in keeping with the aim of this book, it seemed prudent to leave them out. Considering the large amount of changes to the original work, I have chosen to distinguish this edition on its own under the title: *John Cotton: Patriarch of New England.*

It is my sincere hope that the life of John Cotton will inspire this present generation of Christian believers. As with all the American Puritans, they bore flaws and committed sins; the study of their errors ought to act as a warning to those who would unknowingly repeat them. But the American Puritans were remarkable examples of character, courage, and fortitude, worthy of emulation. And John Cotton was perhaps the greatest of them all.

We would do well to heed the exhortation of the apostle Paul as applicable to Rev. Cotton—to follow him as he followed Jesus Christ.

Soli Deo gloria!

Nate Pickowicz
Gilmanton Iron Works, NH
November 2018

General Introduction

A. W. McClure

Veneration for departed worth is a sentiment so natural and proper, that he who is incapable of feeling it must be regarded as hopelessly ungenerous and ignoble. The remembrance of the just is a blessing to them that cherish it. Such memories awaken a pure ambition, and lead to the virtuous resolve to emulate, to equal, to exceed the patterns we admire. The contemplation of exemplary goodness gives life to magnanimous thoughts and beneficent purposes. It is wise to multiply these lessons, and to surround ourselves with these incentives of excellence. The Egyptian graced his habitation with the embalmed persons of his ancestry, hoping that thus their merits might linger in the abode of their descendants. The Grecian multiplied the statues of those who had been distinguished for public or private virtues, believing that the mute eloquence of the sculptured stone would not plead in vain for that respect which ends in imitation. So too let us adorn our dwellings with the memorials of the great and good. Let them be embalmed with the odorous spices of grateful remembrance. Let the very walls of our houses, garnished with their portraits and the pictured story of their deeds, summon us to a righteous emulation. The trophies of Miltiades would not suffer Themistocles to sleep.

As for us whose homes are on the soil of New England, we need not go far from our birthplace to find the most illustrious examples to be studied and copied. Since the days of the apostles, there have been no worthier patterns of Christian character and primitive piety than the Puritans, to whom we are indebted for all that gives our people any superiority in any respect over other nations of the earth. Not that we are to practice an indiscriminate and idolatrous veneration. "There are no errors which are so likely to be drawn into precedent, and therefore none which it is so necessary to expose, as the errors of persons who have a just title to the gratitude and admiration of posterity. In politics, as in religion, there are devotees who show their reverence for a departed saint by converting his tomb into a sanctuary for crime."

But though the Puritans had their faults and failings, what sort of moral appetite must that be which fastens upon and devours these unsavory scraps, and neglects all that is pure and wholesome in their character? If there be any sore spot in their example, these flesh-flies detect it with unerring instinct, and dart upon it with a ravenous delight. He who can see nothing in the sun but its spots must be worse than blind, for while his eye gazes with morbid intensity on darkness, he has no vision for that which is bright and fair.

General Introduction

Luther has said that "evil comes of good," which remark accords with the Rabbinical proverb, "Vinegar is the son of wine." And we find that even some of the descendants of the Puritans have proved so degenerate as, with filial impiety, to blacken and revile the memory of their sires. Foul and unnatural deed! How does it react to the degradation and infamy of its base perpetrators! "There is no readier way," says Tillotson, "for a man to bring his own worth into question, than by endeavoring to detract from the worth of other men." And this is especially the case when the slanderer is vilifying his own progenitors. What can be more odious than to see the child defacing and polluting the sepulcher of his fathers? The only disgrace he can fix upon them is that of having generated a monster so contemptible as himself. Such recreant and apostate natures usually exceed all others in the avidity and malignity with which they traduce the sainted dead. They do this for the reason Dryden gives, and he must have known as being one himself,

> For renegadoes, who ne'er turn by halves,
> Are bound in conscience to be double knaves.[1]

The mists which obscure the sun are exhaled by his own fervent beams. Envy and detraction are the shadows which ever follow shining merit. The calumniators of the Puritans serve as the shades in the picture, which render

---

[1] John Dryden (1631–1700), *Absalom and Achitophel*.

the lights more distinct and vivid. The fair fame of the Puritans shines the more luminous when contrasted with the dark dispositions of their slanderers.

It is but justice to the pious dead to vindicate their good name, which, as Cicero says, is the appropriate possession of the departed. And justice to ourselves requires that we should preserve untarnished the reputation of our fathers, so that we may feel its full influence to quicken our own virtues, and to stimulate them to greater activity and fruitfulness. Certain it is that they will be the most likely to partake of the excellencies of the Puritans who most deeply revere them.

In different ages there have arisen men, too great or too good for the times in which they lived—men, like Israel's martyred prophets, of whom the world was not worthy. They have strode so far in advance of their contemporaries that, as Coleridge said of Milton, they dwarfed themselves in the distance. Bitter scorn and bitterer wrath was their portion while they lived.

And after they are gone, other generations sweep by until the same venerable worthies are again almost lost from view in the dim perspective of the past. Then are their names again decried, because they stopped where they did. The most distinguished of living British essayists has said with a just severity, "It is too much that the benefactors of mankind, after having been reviled by the dunces of their own generation for going too far, are to be reviled by the dunces of the next generation for not going far enough."

The world shows its unworthiness of these good men, either by forgetting their virtues as soon as possible, or else by remembering their names only to traduce them. Thus thanklessly and harshly has it dealt with our pilgrim fathers. But, blessed be the Lord! there are not wanting those, who, like "Old Mortality" among the graves of the Covenanters, with chisel in hand, revisit the resting-place of our Puritan sires, raising up the fallen monuments; removing the encroaching mosses; and, with pious care, retouching the fading inscriptions which the ceaseless stream of time is wearing away.

Such a pleasing task of filial piety and reverent love is before us in the present undertaking. Nor doubt we that the work is well pleasing unto God, who is himself, in his providence, the vindicator of their wisdom and zeal; and whose Word has taught us that the memory of the just is blessed, and that the righteous must be had in everlasting remembrance.

These considerations have induced the Publishing Committee of the Massachusetts Sabbath School Society to prepare a series of biographical sketches of some of the distinguished men, who were God's instruments in making this country what it is. These volumes will collect, and present in one view, everything which relates to them that can be recovered from scattered confusion and from oblivion. It is intended that this exhibition shall bring out the characters, actions, sufferings and principles of these remarkable men, in such form as may interest and profit the general reader, and not be unuseful to such as may be studious of the early history of our country.

The Committee have observed with pain, that there is, in some quarters, a disposition to subject the memory of the Puritans to what is sometimes significantly called "cavalier treatment." The best defense which can be made of these worthies is to show them as they were. Could such an exhibition be made to the life, it is certain that it would have the same dispersing effect upon their detractors, as the appearance of Cromwell's unconquered "Ironsides" had upon the runaways of Naseby, of Preston, and of Worcester.

It is hoped that these volumes will not only find a place in all our Sabbath school libraries, but may obtain a general circulation among the young men and young women of our land. It is believed that the contemplations of these noble examples will be found among the best means of strengthening the minds, enriching the memories, and settling the principles of the young. The moral beauty of the character of the Puritans consist chiefly in this—*they were men of principle*. This made them deliberate in resolving, and inflexible in performing. The "noble grace of decision" shone conspicuously in their lives; they were decided for truth, for conscience, for God. It was a rich gift of the Holy Ghost, and enabled them for a work in which all other adventurers must have failed.

May God bless this undertaking, so that it may help to revive in power and purity the remnants of the piety and spirit of the pilgrims which yet linger among us. May it help to increase the multitudes which, like the Puritans of old, have gone up through much tribulation, from the footstool to the throne!

1
EARLY LIFE & EDUCATION

The man whose life and principles will now be represented, from the vast influence he exercised in his own time and, consequently, upon all following times, has been fitly called "*the Patriarch of New England.*" Boston, especially, is indebted to him for much more than its name. He found it but little better than a woody wilderness, and he left it a flourishing town, a sort of Jerusalem of the West.

Parentage
John Cotton was a native of Derby, on the river Derwent, in England. He was born on the fourth of December, in the year 1585. He was descended of 'gentle blood.' His parents were persons in easy circumstances, and able to provide him with the necessaries for a good education. The father, Roland Cotton, a lawyer by profession, was distinguished, as well as the mother, by a solid and fervid piety. The child, thus brought forth and brought up, did no discredit to his training. His youth, unstained by follies, gave no occasion for reproach in after years. It is

pleasing to consider a person who, from the cradle to the grave, lived a long life without spot or blame, other than what arose from the mistakes of those around him, or those errors of his own which serve to associate him with weak humanity, but not with its vices or its crimes. It is true that, at certain times, amid the tempests of passion and prejudice, much mire and dirt was cast upon his character, but none of it would adhere. It all fell off again, and left his reputation unsullied as ever.

Residence at the University

He was admitted to Trinity College, Cambridge at the early age of thirteen. His father who had never had many clients before, from that time had them in abundance. The son, who had, in consequence, a very liberal maintenance, and who also had a watchful eye to discern the ways of divine providence, was thereby led to say, "God kept me at the university!"

At this ancient seminary, the nursing mother of so many eminent Puritan ministers, he spent fifteen studious years, until he became learned in all the wisdom of that age of erudite scholars and deep divines. He was prevented from obtaining a fellowship in his college, only by reason of embarrassments growing out of the construction of expensive buildings for its use.

After a severe examination, he was then chosen a fellow of Emmanuel College, which he triumphantly sustained. He was examined with special rigor in the Hebrew language. He was tested more particularly upon the latter part of the third chapter of Isaiah, which consists of an inventory of the fineries of the haughty daughters of Zion, such as might well astonish a modern Parisian milliner. This passage, which contains more unusual and perplexing terms than any other in the Old Testament, occasioned no trouble to our ardent scholar, who was able to converse in that tongue. Hebrew literature was much cultivated among the Puritan divines, who gave especial attention to those three languages in which it was stated on the cross, that Jesus of Nazareth was King of the Jews. And yet the famed Erasmus, though reputed in his day to be "the most Greek among the Grecians, and the most Latin among the Latins," and though so used to discourse in the latter language as to forget his mother tongue, gave up the attempt to acquire the Hebrew in utter discouragement.

This study, in which Luther so much delighted, found many expert proficients among the spiritual fathers of New England. Nearly all the first ministers of Massachusetts cultivated it, and some very singular anecdotes are preserved to illustrate their familiarity with that language, which, as John Eliot said, "it pleased our Lord Jesus Christ to make use of when he spoke from heaven unto Paul." Some of the laymen bestowed great attention upon it. Thus Governor Bradford, who had thoroughly mastered some four or five other languages, studied the Hebrew most of all, "because," as he elegantly said, "he would see with his own eyes the ancient oracles of God in their native beauty!"

In the same distinguished College where he gained his fellowship, Mr. Cotton afterwards became Head Lecturer; then Dean, an officer charged to attend to the deportment and discipline of the students; and Catechist, an employment of chief note in the old conventual schools. He was also Tutor to numerous scholars, by whom he was held in the highest estimation as a teacher.

While occupied thus usefully, he was much honored and admired for the strength and readiness of his mind, and for the vast extent of his reading. The sermons, which he occasionally preached in the University, were pompous harangues, stuffed with a huge mass of learning and soaring conceits, according to the taste of the "vain wits" of that seat of science. These ostentatious displays made him very popular with that class of men, who delighted in such parades of learned lore, as much as they distasted the plain preaching of the humbling doctrines of the cross. Cotton was then one of their own sort, being himself of that lamentably numerous class who undertake to preach the gospel of Christ without having personally felt its life and power in the heart.

He first distinguished himself by a funeral discourse for Dr. Some, Master of Peter House, in which he flourished away with so much artificial originality, affected eloquence and "oratorious beauty," that he came to be regarded as the Xenophon of the University, and the special favorite of the muses. Sometime after, he delivered a University sermon in St. Mary's Church, which gained the high applause of the academic pedants, who looked only for a grand exhibition of what the preacher could do to show off himself, rather than for a presentation of "Christ crucified, unto the Jews a stumbling block, and unto the Greeks foolishness; but unto them which are called, both Jews and Greeks, Christ the power of God, and the wisdom of God."[1]

But the Lord had other employment for this "chosen vessel." He who had dwelt so long among those halls of science as one of her most assiduous devotees, began at last to feel the higher claims of religion.

In those days there was at Cambridge an eminent and godly divine, Rev. William Perkins, whose name was long precious among our fathers, one of whom made this epigram upon him, in allusion to a certain natural defect:

> Though nature thee of thy *right* hand bereft,
>   Right well thou writest with thy hand that's *left*.

This good and able man was sound in the faith, and deep in the experience of the great doctrines of the gospel. His ministrations, so searching to the heart and so rousing to the conscience, were blessed to the conversion of many who became some of the brightest lights of their age. Among others, Mr. Cotton was much wrought upon by his faithful exhibition of the truth. But the young and aspiring scholar, fearing to become engaged in the pursuit

---

[1] 1 Corinthians 1:23–24.

of personal religion, lest it should hinder him in the studies he was ambitiously following, suppressed, so far as he could, the motions and stirrings of his mind. In the pride of intellect, and the lust of literary distinction, he resisted the strivings of the Holy Spirit. For a while, he succeeded in stifling the still small voice of conviction, until one day walking in the fields, he heard the bell tolling the death-knell of the devout Mr. Perkins. At this, Mr. Cotton secretly rejoiced, and began to congratulate himself that he should no more be troubled by him, who had, as he said, "laid siege to and beleaguered his heart."

But this selfish satisfaction at such a riddance soon became a cause of great spiritual distress. It dwelt constantly upon his mind as an aggravated sin that he had thus exulted at the prospect of being freed, at such a price, from divine incitements and restraints. God made it "an effectual means of convincing and humbling him in the sight and sense of the natural enmity that is in man's nature against God."[2]

In this state of mind, he heard a sermon from Dr. Sibbes, a man of great note among the Puritans in the time of the first [King] James. This sermon was upon the nature and necessity of regeneration. It first showed the state of the unregenerate, and the misery of those who have no righteousness but that of the moral virtues. Under this discourse, Mr. Cotton felt all his false hopes and

---

[2] Samuel Clark, *A Collection of the Lives of Ten Eminent Divines* (London: William Miller, 1662), 58.

self-righteous confidences failing him. He found the truth of what the Bible taught him, that he was a sinner in the sight of God—that he was wholly and helplessly depraved, and utterly lost beyond the power of recovering himself. For near three years, he was fainting under the burden of desponding thoughts, feeling that he had willfully withstood the means of grace and the offers of mercy which God had extended to him. At length the barbed arrow, which so long had rankled in his heart, was plucked away. Through the same wound from which the bloody drops of contrition had flowed, the healing grace of Jesus was infused. This comfort appears to have been ministered to his soul under the preaching of the same worthy Dr. Sibbes; between whom and the happy convert there ever after subsisted "a singular and constant love," as between a spiritual father and his son in the faith.

Conversion

The conversion of Mr. Cotton was of that primitive, orthodox stamp, which has always produced the best sort of Christians. There is reason to suspect that many who are in the habit of speaking of such a change in terms of levity and unbelief, would inwardly rejoice if they could be assured of undergoing the same moral renovation before they shall be summoned to the bar of God. There is something in such an experience which commends itself even to the conscience of the scoffer and profane. In the case of Mr. Cotton it was no rash and reasonless excitement, but the result of years of anxious inquiry and mental conflict. It occurred when he was at the maturity of his powers and in their highest state of discipline and development. It was a solid work, on a firm foundation, by the Almighty hand, and therefore was it a lasting monument of grace. The subject of it, at the time, was not far from twenty-seven years of age.

A Change of Preaching Style

Before long he was called once more to fill the old stone pulpit of St. Mary's venerable church. A numerous auditory of the University men, attracted by his high reputation, thronged the place. These were hearers, who, as the excellent John Norton said of them, and he knew them well, "prefer the Muses before Moses, and taste Plato more than Paul, and relish the Orator of Athens far above the Preacher of the Cross."[3] They were confidently expecting to be regaled with the heaped up quotations, the philosophical abstractions, the scholastic subtleties, and rhetorical ornaments, by which the preachers on those occasions were wont to hold up to admiration, not their Master, but themselves. When Mr. Cotton arose, the hum of approbation, which used to greet a popular speaker, resounded through the temple. But their expectation was destined to be disappointed. The discourse was upon the subject of *repentance*, and was enunciated from a

---

[3] John Norton, *Memoir of John Cotton* (Boston: Perkins & Marvin, 1834), 31.

heart which had freshly felt the power of the theme. It was a plain, pungent, practical address, directly aimed at the conscience of the hearers. The countenances of his audience betrayed their discontent, in token of which, they pulled down their shovel-caps over their faces, and listened in sullen mood.

The poor preacher, discouraged with this cold reception of his zealous endeavors for their good, retired to his chambers with some sad thoughts of heart. He had not been long alone, when Dr. John Preston, then a fellow of Queen's College, and of great esteem in the University, knocked at his door. This person, like so many others, had repaired to the sermon, with his ears itching to hear a splendid literary performance. For a while, he manifested his vexation in every way he could, but before the close, he was "cut to the heart" by the sword of the Spirit. Making an errand of borrowing a book, he called on Mr. Cotton, with whom he had not been acquainted. His wounded soul could not keep silence, and he sought those spiritual succors which God blessed to the peace of his mind. This man too became a powerful preacher of the gospel, and a mighty man of renown among the Calvinistic doctors of that age of giant minds.

This notable seal of his ministry consoled Mr. Cotton for the manner in which his first evangelical sermon was received by the many. He never regretted that he had cast his ostentatious ways aside, and had sought only to approve himself unto God. Some of the more religious divines prayed him to "persevere in that good way of preaching," which, by the grace of God, he effectually did. How true is the remark of the excellent Thomas Fuller, "It is easier and better for us to please one God than many men with our sermons."[4] Between Mr. Cotton and Dr. Preston there was formed one of those most profitable Christian friendships, which must outlast earth and heaven. There are no good men, but others are the better for them.

---

[4] Thomas Fuller, *The Church History of Britain* (London: Thomas Tegg and Son, 1834), 335.

2
Boston, Lincolnshire

Settlement at Boston in Old England

When Mr. Cotton was about twenty-eight years of age, he was invited by the people of Boston, Lincolnshire to settle in the ministry among them. Old Boston, whose chief honor now is that she imparted her name to her cisatlantic daughter, was indebted for it to Botolph, an ancient Saxon saint; the name 'Botolph's town,' having been, in time, contracted to its present form. In that place, Mr. Cotton labored many years in the pastoral office, exerting a wonderful influence upon the character of the people. We read in Burke's famous speech made long afterwards on American affairs, the odd quotation from an old song—

> Solid men of Boston, make no long orations,
> Solid men of Boston, drink no strong potations.[1]

---

[1] Cited in James Spear Loring, *The Hundred Boston Orators* (Boston: John P. Jewett and Company, 1854), 698.

I am ready to believe that this character for solidity, for brevity of speech, and for observing the "holy dictate of spare temperance," may be owing to the labors of this man of God, leaving their impress upon the descendants of his parishioners there, as I doubt not they have done here.

Obstacles to Settlement

Mr. Cotton's settlement was not without some difficulty. The church-warden, with the better sort of people, desired that he should be their pastor. But the mayor, with the looser class, had procured from Cambridge another candidate more to their minds. When the election came to be held under the charter, the votes were found to be equally divided. The mayor, having the casting vote, by some mistake gave it in favor of Mr. Cotton. The civic dignitary, mortified at his error, requested that the vote might be taken again. His request was complied with, and resulted as before, in an equal division. And now, strange to tell, the mayor made the same mistake, and again gave his casting vote in Mr. Cotton's favor. In great vexation, the blundering magistrate insisted upon trying the vote for the third time, but the people refused their consent. Thus the choice fell upon Mr. Cotton, through the unintended act of his most strenuous opposer.

This obstruction being removed, there came another in the way. Dr. Barlow, the diocesan, understanding that the successful candidate was infected with Puritanism, tried to discourage his settlement. The prelate's only objection was that Mr. Cotton was too young a man to be set over such a numerous and factious people. The young man had so modest an opinion of himself that he was satisfied with the objection, and proposed to go back to the University. But some of his supporters, understanding, as good Mr. Norton tells us, "that one Simon Bibby was to be spoken with, who was near to the bishop, they presently charmed him; and so the business proceeded without further trouble, and Mr. Cotton was admitted into the place after their manner in those days."[2] It looks suspicious in this case that the charmers operated upon the said Simon Bibby, by means of unlawful spells, perchance mingling the potency of *simony* and *bibification*. But whatever the nature of their enchantments may have been, Mr. Cotton cannot be charged with any knowledge of their proceedings.

Spiritual Conflicts

About this time, he was deeply exercised with spiritual troubles, even as his Master was subjected to temptation at the beginning of his public ministry. There is much truth in Luther's saying, "that three things make a divine; meditation, supplication, and temptation."[3] It is probable that few ministers have ever been extensively useful in the

---

[2] Norton, *Memoir*, 34.
[3] Martin Luther (1483-1546), *Table Talk*.

Church of God without first passing through severe conflicts of mind against doubts, and fears, and unbelief; before coming to the settled enjoyment of the consolations and supports of the gospel. Taught both by sterner and by sweeter experience, they learn how to guide others through similar spiritual difficulties. It is thus that they become "able to comfort them which are in any trouble, by the comfort wherewith they themselves are comforted of God."[4]

Engrossed as he was in these severe mental trials, Mr. Cotton paid no heed to the parties and factions which disturbed the town. This sort of impartiality conciliated the good will of the people, when they saw that the salvation of his own soul was far more upon his thoughts, than the contentions and disputes around him.

Arminian Controversy

At that time, there was a Mr. Baron in the place, a man very skillful in his calling as a physician, but who chiefly devoted his studies to the defense of Arminianism, which he maintained, on all occasions, with much acuteness and ability. To his constant conversation, Mr. Cotton silently listened until he "had learned, at length, where all the great strength of the doctor lay."[5] Having mastered all Mr. Baron's scruples and objections and, avoiding all

---

[4] William Burkitt, *Expository Notes on the New Testament* (Yarmouth: Keymer and Co., 1815), 595.

[5] Norton, *Memoir*, 97.

those expressions and phrases of others, which afforded that gentleman any advantage in debate, Mr. Cotton began publicly to preach the doctrine of God's eternal election; the effectual calling of the sinner by irresistible grace; and the certain perseverance of saints, so that they shall not fall from a state of grace, either totally or finally. The result was that the adverse disputant desisted from all further debate; Arminianism died quite away, without struggle or convulsion, "and all matters of religion were carried on calmly and peaceably."[6]

When he had resided at his parish about half a year, he visited Cambridge, to take his degree of Bachelor of Divinity. On this occasion, he added largely to his reputation by a much admired sermon to the clergy, from the text: "Ye are the salt of the earth; but if the salt have lost his savor, wherewith shall it be salted?"[7] He also distinguished himself by his skill in a public disputation, held in the schools for the purpose of proving himself qualified for his degree in divinity. He appeared to high advantage, though matched against a very keen debater, a Dr. Chappell; afterwards Provost of Trinity College in Dublin, and a strenuous advocate of Pelagian sentiments. After gathering these University laurels, Mr. Cotton returned to his parochial charge, where he enjoyed the high esteem of his flock. It is a remark of one of his fellow-laborers, "So God disposeth of the hearts of hearers, as that generally they

---

[6] Norton, *Memoir*, 97.
[7] Matthew 5:13–16.

are all open and loving to their preachers in their first times; trials are often reserved until afterwards. Epiphanius calleth the first year of Christ's ministry, the acceptable year. *Young* Peter girdeth himself, and walks whither he will; but old Peter is girded by another, and carried whither he would not."[8]

Marriage

Being comfortably settled in his church, he married Elizabeth Horrocks, "an eminently virtuous gentlewoman." The day of their union was ever memorable to him upon another account; for it was then that he first received a comfortable assurance of God's love to his soul. The promises of grace and life were sealed upon his heart by the Holy Spirit, and this comfort continued with him, in some happy measure, through the residue of his days. He would often say of the day of his espousals, "God made it a day of double marriage to me!" for it was then that he obtained the blessed evidence of the marriage-union of his soul with Christ.

His worthy companion was of great assistance to him in his ministry, in many respects; but especially in this: that she greatly promoted his usefulness among those of her own sex. The female members of the congregation, taking notice of her uncommon discretion and piety, would freely impart to her the state of their minds upon the subject of religion, acquainting her with their difficulties, and the points on which they stood in need of special

---

[8] Attributed to John Norton.

counsel and instruction. The information she imparted to her husband, enabled him to adapt his public teaching to the wants of his hearers, and to render it far more conducive to their spiritual good.

If experience can prove anything, it has abundantly proved that the judicious marriage of a clergyman greatly enhances his usefulness, and his estimation among his flock. It not only places him as "a family man," in close sympathy with the families of his flock, but it puts him in unexceptionable communication with the female portion of his charge. He thus obtains a sufficiently confidential knowledge of the condition of their minds, and also the opportunity of meeting their wants as a religious shepherd and guide. He in this manner becomes qualified to benefit them, far beyond what it would be practicable or desirable to do by means of personal familiar intercourse. It is not without reason, that the Apostle gives repeated counsel, that every elder or parochial bishop, should be "the husband of one wife,"[9] neither more nor less.

Non-Conformity

After Mr. Cotton had spent three years in Boston, his deep and devout studies brought him to a solemn conviction that there were many antiquated corruptions yet left unreformed in the national Church with the practice of which he could not comply. From this time, he ceased to

---

[9] 1 Timothy 3:2.

conform strictly to the Church of England, though he never voluntarily renounced its communion.

3
Persecutions & Translation

Countenanced by the People in His Non-Conformity

When Mr. Cotton ceased from his conformity with the exceptionable features in the national worship, so great was his popularity with his people that, far from opposing him on that account, the greatest part of them sustained him in his course. Thomas Leverett, however, one of his parishioners, with some others, prosecuted complaints against their minister in the Episcopal courts until, after some time, he was silenced by order of the bishop.

Suspension from Ministry

During his suspension, Mr. Cotton gave constant attendance to the public preaching of his substitute, but never to the reading of the Book of Common Prayer. He was now subjected to severe temptations to swerve from the path of duty. He was not only promised that he should be restored to the freedom of his ministry, but promoted to very great preferment in the church, on condition of conformity to the scrupled rites, only in a single instance. But he kept the integrity of his conscience undefiled, "unawed by influence, and unbribed by gain."[1]

Meanwhile a portentous cloud of troubles was gathering over his head, but was strangely dispersed again. Mr. Leverett himself, the author of these difficulties, became deeply penitent for his agency in causing them. He went to one of the proctors of the archi-episcopal court, to whom he presented a pair of gloves, and then made his appeal from the court below. Mr. Leverett made oath before this officer, who favored him in the terms of the deposition, that "Mr. Cotton was a man conformable *to the mind of the Lord.*" On the strength of this very ambiguous deposition, the silenced minister, he scarce knew how, found himself healed of his ecclesiastical bronchitis, and restored to the use of his voice in the pulpit. The same Mr. Leverett ever after was his steadfast friend, and following his fortunes to this side of the Atlantic, was for many years a useful elder in the first church in Boston, Massachusetts. By the same means, Mr. Bennet, another of his parishioners, occasionally screened his minister from harassing prosecutions.

Successful Labors

After this affair, Mr. Cotton went on with his sacked duties, uninterrupted for many years. Making no efforts to

---

[1] T. J. Sawyer and P. Price, eds., *The Christian Messenger*, vol. 1 (New York: P. Price, 1832), 16.

build up a party or to gain adherents, he laboriously devoted himself to teaching the people the Christian religion. During the twenty years that he retained his charge, he thrice went over the whole body of systematic divinity, with special pains to indoctrinate the younger part of his flock. In his preaching he largely expounded several of the books of Scripture, in which gift he greatly excelled.

As one instance of his power to awaken the conscience, it is said that he once handled the sixth commandment with such effect that a woman who had been married sixteen years to her second husband, openly confessed to the crime of poisoning her former husband. This confession she made, though it exposed her to be burned to death at the stake, the barbarous punishment then awarded to such an offense, which was regarded as "petty treason."

Theological Instructions

So great was Mr. Cotton's celebrity as an instructor that his house was full of young students, some of whom resorted to him from Holland, and some from Germany. In those days, the sons of the Puritans did not repair to the land where too many of the learned, enveloped in the fumes of their unquenchable pipes, "drink beer and think beer," until their brains reek with the noisome smoke of transcendental speculation. The most of Mr. Cotton's pupils were from that University where he had been trained, for Dr. Preston ever counseled his students who had nearly completed the prescribed course of studies, to perfect their preparation for public services by a brief residence with the puritan minister of Boston. It came to be a common saying that, "Mr. Cotton is Dr. Preston's seasoning vessel."

Indefatigable Preaching

His ministerial labors were abundant. In addition to the ordinary duties of the Sabbath, he preached statedly four times in the week, *viz.*, early each Wednesday and Thursday morning, and again in the afternoons of Thursday and Saturday. Moreover he frequently held other occasional services, in which he often spent six hours in prayer and preaching. When we think of such immense labors sustained through a long course of years, we are at a loss which to admire most; the indefatigable industry of the teacher, or the insatiable eagerness of the people for his instructions. In these degenerate days, such congregations are as rare as such ministers. For several of the latter years of his residence in that well cultured field, he was assisted by a colleague. That was not the era of superabounding periodicals and cheap literature. The mass of the people then depended on hearing, for mental aliment and excitement, as much as now on reading.

Correspondence

Mr. Cotton's usefulness was further extended by a large correspondence with those who sought his aid for resolving obscure points of doctrine, difficult texts of Scripture, or perplexing cases of conscience. Besides this he was considerably occupied every year in providing for the spiritual wants of other congregations, and especially in his native place, where he was held in the highest estimation.

Wonderful & General Reformation

The multiplied toils of this faithful servant were not thrown away. The Spirit of the Lord was with him. There was a surprising reformation of manners in the community. Profaneness was well nigh abolished. Hurtful and superstitious practices were done away. The great body of the people became decidedly religious. As the phrase was, most of the *Satanicals* had become *Puritanicals*. The mayor, with the greater part of the magistrates, had embraced the truth. Many scores of devout persons, without forming themselves into a separate church, more fully perfected their existing church-state by solemnly covenanting with God and with each other, to follow the Lord in the purity of his worship. The minister whose fidelity was thus rewarded, was the admiration of his hearers, "exceedingly beloved of the best, and admired and reverenced of the worst."[2] He was held in high respect by some of the chief dignitaries both in Church and State. It was noticed that the temporal prosperity of the town was

---

[2] Thomas Hutchinson, *A Collection of Original Papers Relative to the History of the Colony of Massachusetts Bay* (Boston: Thomas and John Fleet, 1769), 246.

much promoted by the increased intelligence and good order which pervaded the place in consequence of his activity. On his account it was much resorted to by strangers, and "many gentlemen of good quality" made it their abode.

At this time, Mr. Cotton had a very able colleague. Dr. Anthony Tuckney, afterwards Master of St. John's College, Cambridge. While he filled this latter office, he published a *Briefe Exposition of Ecclesiastes*, by Mr. Cotton, a year or two subsequent to the latter's decease. To this volume, printed at London in 1654, Dr. Tuckney prefixed a dedication, addressed to the mayor, with the aldermen and other Christian friends of Boston, Lincolnshire. The dedication presents a very happy picture of his joint ministry with Mr. Cotton in that favored place. "The large interest," says Dr. Tuckney, "which I have long enjoyed in your favor, and which you must ever have in my heart, hath emboldened me to prefix your names to this piece; and with the more confidence of its acceptance, because in it an address is made to you at once by *two* who sometimes were together your ministers in the gospel of Christ: by the ever to be honored Mr. Cotton, in the book, and by my unworthy self in the review and dedication of it. Both of us are now removed from you: the one, first to a remote part of the world, there to plant churches and thence, after that happy work done, to heaven; the other to some more public service nearer hand. I often call to mind those most comfortable days, in which I enjoyed the happiness of joint ministry with so able and faithful a guide: and both of us so much satisfaction and encouragement from a people so united in the love both of the truth, and of one another. I cannot read what Paul writeth of his Thessalonians (in the first chapters of both his epistles to them), but I think I read over what we then found in Boston. They were then very happy days with you, when your faith did grow exceedingly, and your love to Christ's ordinances, ministers, servants, and to one another abounded. Although your town be situated in a low country, yet God then raised your esteem very high: and your eminency in piety overtopped the height of your steeple. Your name was as an ointment poured out, and your renown went forth for that beauty and comeliness, which God had put upon you."[3]

How can we refrain from lamenting that a Christian flock, so happily and profitably united under the guidance of its beloved pastors, could not escape the fury of religious tyranny? Such interference is impotent as to any good, but all powerful for evil. There is evidence that the leaven of Mr. Cotton's piety long lingered in that once favored place. Perhaps we have an evidence that its influence is still, in some measure, transmitted to the present inhabitants. In this year, 1846, the mayor and aldermen of that ancient corporation addressed a letter to the civic authorities of Boston in New England. This well-written communication was sent with the noble design of drawing closer the bonds of amity between two countries which

---

[3] John Cotton, *A Brief Exposition of Ecclesiastes* (London, 1654).

were apprehended to be in some danger of coming to hostilities. In this friendly missive, the people of the mother town do not fail to remind the trans-atlantic daughter, that she is indebted to them of old for their famous Mr. Cotton, and their more famous name. From thence is drawn an argument for the peace of the nations to which these cities respectively belong.

Archbishop Williams

His learning, and his ability in putting it to good use, made him a special favorite with Archbishop Williams. And when that prelate was bishop of Lincoln, and also Lord Keeper of the Great Seal, being the last ecclesiastic who held that office in England, he went to the imperious James I, and made so favorable a report of Mr. Cotton's singular worth and learning, that the king gave consent that his ministry should not be interrupted on account of his non-conformity. And this was very remarkable when we consider that monarch's impetuosity and exasperation against such as offended in that particular. The mystery of Mr. Cotton's impunity was not known to Samuel Ward, of facetious memory, the author of the "Simple Cobbler." He remarked in his pleasant manner, "Of all men in the world, I envy Mr. Cotton of Boston most; for he does nothing by way of conformity, and yet has his liberty; and I do almost everything that way, and cannot enjoy mine."[4]

Earls of Dorchester & Lindsay

The vicar of Boston was very much respected by the earls of Dorchester and Lindsay. These noblemen being in the vicinity, attending to the draining of some part of the Lincolnshire fens, came to hear this noted preacher. His text that day was Galatians 2:20, "I am crucified with Christ," &c.; and he was prepared to discourse on the duty of living by faith in adversity. But considering that these high and mighty lords had never been very conversant with adversity, he promptly reversed his subject, and expatiated on the duty of living by faith in prosperity. It is said, that they also heard him discourse on civil government, and were greatly captivated with the wisdom and spirit by which he spoke. They assured him of their friendship, and offered, if ever it should be needed, to exert all their influence at the royal court in his behalf. When these puissant nobles had occasioned some scandal by indulging in diversions unsuitable to the Sabbath, they kindly accepted his discreet admonitions, and promised reformation. His faithful dealing is the more to be commended, when we consider the profound veneration then felt for those who

---

[4] Alexander Young, *Chronicles of the First Planters of the Colony of Massachusetts Bay, from 1623 to 1636* (Boston: Charles C. Little and James Brown, 1846), 426-427.

were so favored in the accident of birth. We have heard old countrymen, advanced in years, tell of the awful respect in which nobility was held in their young days, so that, in attempting to speak to a peer of the realm with his star upon his breast, the tongue would cleave to the roof of the mouth.[5] The French Revolution seems to have forever broken down this feeling of overpowering veneration for aristocracy. We look upon an anointed king with far less emotion in these times, when reverence for mere rank is rapidly passing away.

Disabled by Ague & Second Marriage

Toward the end of his residence in Boston, Mr. Cotton was for a whole year disabled from preaching by a quartern ague, which began in September, 1630. His physicians advising a change of air, he removed to the mansion of the earl of Lincoln, another of his noble friends whose Countess was a lady of eminent piety. Among their children was the celebrated lady Arbella Johnson, and also the lady Susan, wife of John Humphrey, one of the assistants. Both of these ladies settled, and the former died, in this colony of Massachusetts. In the hospitable dwelling of their parents, Mr. Cotton recovered his health, but lost his estimable wife by the same disease, after a happy and

---

[5] It was said, that a young lady from the country being ushered into the dread presence of Sarah, Duchess of Marlborough, lost all her self-possession, and falling upon her knees, mechanically recited her customary grace at meals: "Lord, make us suitably thankful for what we are about to receive!"

religious union of eighteen years. About a year after, he married an estimable widow, Mrs. Sarah Story, who was an endeared friend of his former wife. Good Mr. Norton, speaking of these grave and godly matrons, compares them with Euodias and Syntyche, "which labored with Paul in the gospel."

Cited to High Commission Court
Not long after his second marriage, the tempest, which had been delayed for so many years, broke forth. There was in the town a dissipated character, Gawain Johnson by name, whose irregularities had brought him under the notice of the correctional police. Resolved to be revenged upon the magistrates by whom he had been punished, he went up to London, and filed an information against them in that infamous tribunal, the High Commission Court. This body was styled the "High Commissioners for Causes Ecclesiastical," and was first set up by Queen Elizabeth in 1559. It was composed of bishops, privy counselors, officers of state, lawyers, deans, and the like, to the number of forty or more; three of whom, usually with a bishop, or other dignitary, at their head, were vested with full power to inquire into and punish all opinions or practices different from those of the established Church. All such cases they could try, either with or without a jury, the whole supremacy and despotism of the monarch being committed into their hands by royal commission. Persons informed against by letter only were cited before them, and in trying them, no regard was had to the statute laws

of the realm. The accused were tossed about in the vast, stormy and most uncertain gulf of the common law; where shipwreck was almost inevitable.

The most odious of the proceedings in that court, in which witnesses were not openly examined, was the oath *ex officio*—an oath by which the prisoner was required to answer any question which should be put to him, no matter how deeply the answer might injure him. If he refused to swear, he was severely punished for contempt of court; if he answered, he was convicted on his own confession. This outrage was systematically committed against every principle of law and justice, requiring that no man shall be compelled to criminate himself. Hume has justly denounced the High Commission as a "real Inquisition; attended with similar iniquities and cruelties."[6] Dr. Lingard, himself a Romanist, says: "The chief difference consisted in their names. One was the court of Inquisition, the other of High Commission."[7] This tribunal, while it lasted, was in truth a very efficient substitute for the Inquisition, which Du Plessis Mornay energetically called, "that hell of the papacy."

Fate of the Informer

The charge made at the office of this infamous court against the Boston magistrates was for not kneeling at the

---

[6] David Hume, *The History of England* (Dublin: United Company of Booksellers, 1775).

[7] John Lingard, *A History of England*, vol. 7 (Philadelphia: Eugene Cummisky, 1827), 60.

sacrament, and for neglecting some other ceremonies of the like importance. The officers of the court required that the minister's name should be inserted. "Nay," said the informer, Johnson, "the minister is an honest man, and never did me any wrong." But being told that his complaint would be thrown out unless it included the name of the minister who permitted the alleged irregularities, the miserable man, rather than lose his revenge, inserted the name of one who had never injured him. Upon this, letters missive were forthwith dispatched to bring Mr. Cotton before that dreaded bar.

The Rev. John Rogers of Dedham, England, one of the sons of that Marian martyr who used to be figured in the rude wood cuts of the New England Primer, was informed of the accusation entered against Mr. Cotton. Mr. Rogers received the sorrowful tidings just as he was going to preach his weekly lecture. In his discourse he deeply lamented the occurrence, and broke out, with a sort of prophetic fire, in words to this effect: "As for that man who hath caused a faithful pastor to be driven from his flock, he is a wisp used by the hand of God for the scouring of his people. But mark the words now spoken by a minister of the Lord! I am verily persuaded that the judgments of God will overtake the man that hath done this thing; either he will die under a hedge, or something else, more than the ordinary death of men, shall befall him."[8]

---

[8] Norton, *Memoir*, 98.

Those old men of God did not hesitate to venture a prediction of this kind, for they had full often witnessed the wretched end of such characters:

> And old experience doth attain,
>   To something like prophetic strain.[9]

And it came accordingly to pass that this sorry informer, very shortly after, died of the plague under a hedge in Yorkshire. Through fear of contagion, he perished alone, and was left long unburied. Our fathers, who were exceedingly inquisitive and trustful in such matters, did not fail to recognize in this event an evident divine retribution from the hand of Him, who, as the Psalmist says, "hath bent his bow, and made it ready, who ordaineth his arrows against the persecutors."[10]

Good Mr. Whiting, "the angel of the church in Lynn," where he was the first pastor, was himself a native of old Boston. He wrote a biographical sketch of Mr. Cotton, which was the basis of John Norton's more extended memoir, on which latter work Cotton Mather enlarged considerably. To the facts related in Mather's very valuable account, the present narrative makes very great additions collected from every available source. This Mr. Whiting, speaking of John Cotton's enemies, who secretly plotted, or openly acted, against him in old Boston,

---

[9] John Milton (1608–1674), *Il Penseroso*, lines 173–174.
[10] Psalm 7:13.

remarks: "They all of them were blasted, either in their names, or in their estates, or in their families, or in their devices, or else came to untimely deaths; which shows how God hath owned his servant in his holy labors; and that in the things wherein they dealt proudly against him, he would be above them."[11] Doubtless, the avenging providence of God is not to be rashly scrutinized. We cannot be too cautious in the interpretation of such matters. And yet a broad induction of facts will justify the solemn conclusion, that "verily there is a God that judgeth in the earth." His people are his charge. "Yea, he hath reproved kings for their sakes, saying, 'Touch not mine anointed, and do my prophets no harm.'"[12]

Concealment

Mr. Cotton, warned that letters missive were issued against him, concealed himself from the easier search of the pursuivants by flight. He was aware that, if apprehended, he had nothing better to expect than to pine in perpetual imprisonment, in which so many of his brethren had worn out their shortened days. During his concealment, his potent friend, the Earl of Dorchester, or as more commonly called, Dorset, who was a thorough courtier, lord chamberlain to the Queen, and far enough from being

---

[11] Samuel Whiting, "Concerning the Life of the Famous Mr. Cotton" in *Chronicles of the First Planters of the Colony of Massachusetts Bay, 1623-1636* (Boston: Charles C. Little and James Brown, 1846), 427.

[12] 1 Chronicles 16:22.

a Puritan, exerted all his influence in the case. But that grinding and remorseless oppressor, Laud, who, about this time, was made archbishop of Canterbury, and who on the very day that he became primate and metropolitan of all England, received, by a significant coincidence, the offer of a cardinal's hat from Rome, was inexorable. That bitter prelate would often exclaim: "that I could meet with Cotton!" The noble earl, perceiving that all his intercessions must be unavailing, wrote to the irreproachable fugitive, that "if he had been guilty of drunkenness, or uncleanness, or any such *lesser* fault, he could have obtained his pardon, but inasmuch as he had been guilty of non-conformity and puritanism, the crime was unpardonable,"[13] and ended with advising him to fly for his safety. It is not surprising, after this sample of their quality, that Mr. Cotton should long after say:

> The ecclesiastical courts are like the courts of the high priests and Pharisees, which Solomon, by a spirit of prophecy stileth, dens of lions and mountains of leopards. And those who have to do with them, have found them markets of the sins of the people, the cages of uncleanness, the forges of extortion, the tabernacles of bribery.[14]

---

[13] Cited in Samuel Gardner Drake, *The History and Antiquities of the City of Boston*, vol. 1. (Boston: Luther Stevens, 1854), 160.

[14] Cited in *Publications of the Narragansett Club*, vol. 2 (Providence: Providence Press Company, 1867), 140.

Letter to Mrs. Cotton

There is extant a letter, dated October 3, 1632, written by Mr. Cotton while under concealment, to the lady he had but lately married. It is here inserted as presenting a confidential expression of his feelings at the time.

> Dear &c. If our heavenly Father be pleased to make our Yoke more heavy than we did so soon expect, remember I pray thee what we have heard, that our heavenly Husband the Lord Jesus, when he first called us to Fellowship with himself, called us unto this Condition, to deny ourselves, and to take up our Cross daily, to follow him. And truly, though this Cup be brackish at the first; yet a Cup of God's mingling is doubtless sweet in the Bottom, to such as have learned to make it their greatest Happiness to partake with Christ, as in his Glory, so in the Way that leadeth to it. Where I am for the present, I am very fitly and welcomely accommodated, I thank God: so as I see here I might rest desired enough till my Friends at Home shall direct further. They desire also to see thee here, but that I think it not safe yet, till we see how God will deal with our Neighbours at Home: for if you should now travel this Way, I fear you will be watched and dogged at the Heels. But I hope shortly God will make Way for thy safe Coming. The Lord watch over

you all for Good, and reveal himself in the Guidance of all our Affairs. So with my Love to thee, as myself, I rest; desirous of thy Rest and Peace in him.

J. C.[15]

This letter, written under such circumstances of painful separation, imminent peril, and uncertainty for the future, betrays no petulant impatience or unmanly repinings. It beautifully portrays the sublime peacefulness of the mind, which, in the hour of adversity, is stayed on God. Within six weeks from the writing of the above letter, this pious couple was again united, though obliged still to live in concealment.

Sets Out to Go to Holland

After earnest prayer for divine direction, and much consultation with good men upon the subject, Mr. Cotton concluded to seek refuge in Holland, whither so many of the Puritan ministers and people had already fled from the violence of persecution. Some of his Boston friends urged him to permit them to sustain and protect him, that they might privately enjoy the benefit of his ministry, without which they must be exposed to great temptation. But the venerable Mr. Dod, an old Puritan famous for his piety and his wit, told them, "that the removing of a minister

---

[15] Young, *Chronicles*, 432.

was like the draining of a fish-pond; the good fish will follow the water; but eels, and other refuse fish, will stick in the mud."[16]

That there were in the pond some good fish, with life enough to follow the water, appears from Mr. Cotton's book on the *Holinesse of Church-Members*, printed many years after in 1650. It is dedicated "to my honored, worshipful and worthy friends, the Mayor and Justices, the Aldermen and Common Council, together with the whole Congregation and Church at Boston." Speaking of old times with them, he says:

> And ye became followers of us, and of the Lord; and showed yourselves examples in some first fruits of reformation, unto many neighbor congregations about you: 1 Thess. 1:6, 7. And though you saw, that any small measure of reformation, (which then was offensive to the State, and suffered under the name of NON-CONFORMITY) would expose yourselves to some sufferings, unless you deserted me, yet I bear you record, you chose rather to expose yourselves to charge and hazard for many years together, than to expose my ministry to silence.
>
> And though, at last, in that hour and power of darkness, when the late High Commission began to stretch forth their malignant arm against us, I was forced to depart secretly from you, (from some of you, I say) howbeit, not without

---

[16] Cited in Mather, *Magnalia*, 241.

the privity and consent of the chief, yet sundry of you yielded up yourselves, as Ittai to David, to follow the Lord whithersoever he should call; and to go along with me, whether to life or death, in this late howling wilderness. And though, after my departure, you were somewhat carried aside with the torrent of the times, yet, I believe, not without some apprehension of the light of the word going before you, in your judgments, to the satisfaction of your own consciences. And ever since that time, wherein the strong hand of the Lord, and the maglignancy of the times, had set this vast distance of place, and great gulf of seas, between us; yet still you claimed an interest in me, and have yearly ministered some real testimony of your love.

And at last, when the Lord, of his rich grace, had dispelled the storm of malignant church-government, you invited me again and again, to return unto the place and work wherein I had walked before the Lord and you in former times. But the estate of those of you who came along with me, and who thereby had most interest in me, could not bear that. Nor would my relation to the church here suffer it. Nor would my age, now stricken in years, nor infirm body, ill-brooking the seas, be able to undergo it, without extreme peril of becoming unserviceable either to yourselves or others.[17]

---

[17] John Cotton, *On the Holiness of Church Members* (London, 1650), iv.

From this document we learn several things, which might not otherwise have come to our knowledge. It appears that the affections of his old flock clung to their banished minister; and that, through some twenty years of absence, they annually sent him substantial tokens of their anxiety to promote his comfort. We find too, that when the execution of William Laud and Charles Stuart had removed the bar to his return, they sent him such reiterated and urgent calls as could be declined only for the most imperative reasons.

To these reasons there is another to be added. While the Long Parliament was at the height of its power, before Cromwell had dosed it with his "purging colonels," the presbyterial form of government was imposed by law on the parishes of England. Presbyterianism, at that time, admitted persons confessedly unregenerate to the Lord's Table. In reference to this, Mr. Cotton told his importunate friends:

> The estate of your church, admitting more than professed saints to the fellowship of the seals, and the government of your church subjected to an extrinsical ecclesiastical power, would have been perpetual scruples and torments to my conscience, which, knowing the terrors of the Lord, and the conviction of my own judgment, I durst not venture upon.

To this he adds, in his charitable, unreproaching manner:

Not that I misjudge others who can satisfy their consciences in a larger latitude; but because every man is to be fully persuaded in his own mind, and I must live by my own faith (Rom. 14:5).

Mr. Cotton did not lay down his pastoral charge in any summary or informal manner. He first obtained the consent of his people, so far as it was possible to consult them on the subject. "On this point," he says,

I conferred with the chief of our people, and offered them to bear witness to the truth I had preached and practiced amongst them, even unto bonds, if they conceived it might be any confirmation to their faith and patience. But they dissuaded me from that course, and thinking it better for themselves, and for me, and for the Church of God, to withdraw myself from the present storm, and to minister in this country [New England, whence this letter was written] to such of their town as they had sent before hither, and such others as were willing to go along with me, or to follow after me.[18]

Governor Hutchinson has preserved for us a letter[19] to Dr. Williams, Bishop of Lincoln, written by Mr. Cot-

---

[18] See letter dated December 3, 1634, in Thomas Hutchinson (1711-1780), *Original Papers*.

[19] See letter dated May 7, 1633, in Hutchinson, *Original Papers*.

ton, a few weeks before sailing for America, for the purpose of resigning his vicarage into the prelate's hands. Dr. Williams had showed him all the indulgence he could, until Laud compelled the reluctant prelate to resort to rigorous measures. Mr. Cotton gratefully acknowledges the diocesan's kindness, gives a short account of the drift of his ministry at Boston, and assigns the reasons of his departure in a manner the most meek and respectful, and yet happily blended with a high-principled firmness and religious independence. This communication breathes the deepest solicitude for the welfare of the flock from which he was torn away.

Diverted to London
Being thus fully released from all obligation of duty to his recent charge, he took measures to effect his escape from his native shores. To shun the officers who were on the watch for his apprehension, he traveled under an assumed name and a change of garb, toward the port where he expected to embark for Holland. But when he had nearly reached the place, he was met by one of his relatives, who, by dint of persuasion and entreaty, induced him to betake himself to London.

Interesting Conference with Mr. Davenport & Others
There were then in that city three pious ministers who considered the imposed ceremonies as things in themselves of little consequence, and as such submitted to

them. One of these was Dr. Goodwin, a clergyman of great distinction, and afterwards one of the leading divines in the renowned Westminster Assembly. The cynical Anthony Wood styles him and Dr. Owen, "the two Atlasses and Patriarchs of Independency." Another of the three alluded to was Mr. Thomas Nye, in high repute for learning. The other was John Davenport, the founder of the New Haven colony, and one of the "chief fathers" of New England. These gentlemen embraced the opportunity of holding a conference with Mr. Cotton. Knowing him to be an exceedingly dispassionate and judicious man, they made no doubt but that they should convince him that it was his duty to conform rather than to leave his country and his flock.

At this conference he first confuted all the arguments they could array to justify their conformity, and then vindicated his own course in choosing to undergo so great privations, rather than to defile his conscience by acquiescing in customs which derogated from the kingly office of the great Head of the Church. As the result of these discussions, these three able champions came entirely over to Mr. Cotton's views. Nor does this detract at all from their just reputation, but rather enhances it. "For he that is overcome of the truth parteth victory with him that overcometh, and hath the best share for his own part." These men belonged to that class of which good Fuller says, that "they count themselves the greatest conquerors, when the truth hath taken them captive."[20] The three, not long after, themselves became exiles for the truth to which they had honorably yielded."[21] After Mr. Cotton's death, Mr. Davenport gave a glowing account of this interesting debate, in which he says, Mr. Cotton "answered with great evidence of Scripture light, composedness of mind, mildness of spirit, constant adhering to his principles, and keeping them unshaken."[22]

The trio of friends in this amicable contention were struck with admiration at his might in the Scriptures, his vast and various reading, his prompt memory, his ready reply, and his government of his own spirit, far beyond what they had "taken notice of in any man before him." Mr. Davenport closes by saying, "The reason of our desire to confer with him rather than any other touching these weighty points was our former knowledge of his approved godliness, excellent learning, sound judgment, eminent gravity, candor and sweet temper of spirit, whereby he could placidly bear those that differed from

---

[20] Thomas Fuller, *The Holy and Profane State* (Boston: Little, Brown and Company, 1864), 89–90.

[21] This Dr. Goodwin lay wind-bound, in hourly expectation that the pursuivants would seize him before the wind would favor his escape to Holland. Distressed as he was for a more propitious gale, he cried, "Lord, if thou hast at this time any poor servant of thine who wants this wind more than I do another, I do not ask for the changing of it: I submit unto it." The wind soon came about, and carried him clear from his pursuers.

[22] Cited in Norton, *Memoir*, 62.

him in their apprehensions. All which, and much more we found; and glorified God, in him, and for him."[23] This description explains the secret of Mr. Cotton's uncommon success as a debater, and as a resolver of the doubtful and difficult questions in his casuistry which were constantly submitted to him for solution. Truly, these men who are so firmly tenacious of their opinions, and yet thus maintain them in the spirit of love and the meekness of wisdom, are usually the most invincible and irresistible in debate.

In John Cotton's *Covenant of Grace*, a book written long after this in America, of which several editions were printed, there is, in that of 1655, an Address to the reader by Rev. Thomas Allen, minister of St. Edward's, Norwich, England, who a few years before had been teacher of the church in Charlestown, Massachusetts. The addresser says of the author, "He was a man of peace, of a very sweet spirit, and had a very special faculty of composing differences in the judgments of the brethren. And thus much I shall crave liberty to testify of him, that, besides the multiplicity of occasions which was constantly upon him, he was not without care about the peace and welfare of the churches abroad; and notwithstanding his so vast a distance in body from the churches and saints in his native country, yet he had great thoughts in heart for the division of his brethren here, being seriously studious

---

[23] Norton, *Memoir*, 62–63.

how to compose and heal their breaches. He hath sometimes said unto me, being privately together: 'Brother, I perceive there is a great *gravamen* which the one party is much offended at with the other. I pray let us study how we may ease and remove it.'"[24]

Mr. Whiting gives him this character as a disputant: "He was of admirable candor, of unparalleled meekness, of rare wisdom, very loving even to those that differed in judgment from him, yet one that held his own stoutly, tightly maintaining and keenly defending what himself judged to be the truth."[25] Beware of such men, unless you be willing to accord with them.

It is worth mentioning here that, among the auditors in that London conference was Rev. Henry Whitfield, rector of Oakley in Surrey, who from that time became a conscientious non-conformist, and was afterwards the founder of the town and church of Guilford, in the New Haven colony.

Resolves to Go to New England

While secreted at London, by Mr. Davenport and other ministers, Mr. Cotton gave up the design of proceeding to Holland. He was discouraged from betaking himself to that country, for the same reasons which induced Mr. Robinson's Leyden flock to leave it for America. Letters

---

[24] John Cotton, *Treatise on the Covenant of Grace*.
[25] Samuel Whiting, "Famous Mr. Cotton," in Young, *Chronicles of the First Planters*, 425.

from Governor Winthrop, and from the infant church in our own Boston, decided him to shun the fires of persecution by braving the waters of the ocean, then much more formidable to the voyager than now.

It was about the middle of July 1633, when Mr. Cotton, with Thomas Hooker and Samuel Stone, two ministers of great note, and with a number of his old Boston parishioners, commenced his adventurous voyage. They sailed in a vessel called the *Griffin*, the name of a fabled creature, partly eagle and partly lion. It was a ship of three hundred tons, having at this time about two hundred passengers, of whom four died while on the way.

Embarks with Difficulty in the Griffin

Mr. Cotton and Mr. Hooker experienced much difficulty in getting out of England, for long search had been made for them by the emissaries of that odious instrument of all sorts of tyranny, the High Commission Court. All the ports were waylaid for their apprehension, and at the Isle of Wight, where it was expected that the *Griffin* would have made her last stoppage, she was strictly searched by the pursuivants. But the staunch ship afterwards, by private agreement, lay off the Downs, and, griffin-like, with lion heart and eagle wings, swooped upon the prey, and bore it in triumph from the disappointed hunters.

But oh, the sadness of that hour! when the hapless exiles, relieved at last from the haunting fear of capture, felt all their love of home rise in the strength of that mastering passion. Forgetting the bitterness of their lot, and regardless of the hardships of the future, they wept their last farewell to parted friends, and to the native land they should see no more. Natural affection was strong, but gracious affection was stronger. The love of Christ constrained them. God counted their bitter tears, and they have found them each a pearl in heaven. "And Jesus answered and said, 'Verily I say unto you, there is no man that hath left house, or brethren, or sisters, or father, or mother, or wife, or children, or lands, for my sake and the gospel's, but he shall receive an hundred-fold now in this time, houses, and brethren and sisters, and mothers, and children, and lands, with persecutions; and in the world to come, eternal life.'"[26]

We almost envy our fathers for their distressing opportunity of evincing the strength, sincerity and purity of their love to Jesus, before they went to meet him joyfully at his judgment-seat. And is there no way, in which the tenderness and constancy of our love may be put to decisive proof? Can we do nothing to show that our hearts are wholly given to the Lord? Aye, by crucifying our bosom-sins, by pure and holy living, by unremitted efforts for the salvation of men, by our utmost exertions to promote the Church's grand mission work of the world's conversion, by ceaseless sacrifices joyfully made in the holy cause of benevolence, by these, we too may prove that Jesus has full possession of our souls. Thus may we make it mani-

---

[26] Luke 18:30.

fest, that, in blood and in spirit, we are the sons of the pilgrims. This shall argue for us, that we are ready, if persecution should arise, to suffer what our fathers endured—that we are ready to walk, like them, with firm, unfaltering step, through pains and perils for conscience' sake; that we are ready to follow on, through despoilment, exile, bonds and death, to the celestial throne, and the crown eternal.

4
Boston, Massachusetts

Voyage to America

It was about the middle of July 1633, when Mr. Cotton commenced his voyage. Both he and Mr. Hooker preserved their disguise until they were so far over the main ocean that they could safely disclose who they were. Mr. Stone, who was much the youngest, and for whom the search was not so furious, performed all the public religious duties of the ship's company until his companions could resume their character as preachers, and officiate in their turns.

This was a richly freighted ship, bearing a large part of the fortune of New England. Our pun-loving ancestors observed, at her coming, that God had supplied them with three necessary commodities: "*Cotton* for their clothing, *Hooker* for their fishing, and *Stone* for their building." During the voyage, they usually had three services every day, which was, perhaps, the first example of a "protracted meeting."

Birth of Seaborn Cotton

When they had been a month at sea, Mr. Cotton, whose first wife died childless, became a father. This, his eldest child, received the name *Seaborn*, in commemoration of the mercies attending his birth. Seaborn Cotton lived to be a highly useful and honored minister of the gospel. There were other children born on the same passage. At the end of seven weeks, which was then regarded as a remarkably expeditious and prosperous voyage, they landed at what is now the good old city of Boston on the third day of September, 1633.

This place had then been settled three years. Governor Dudley says that the first settlers, previous to their coming hither, had already determined to name the place they should fix upon after the scene of Mr. Cotton's pastoral labors, and in compliment to him, with the hope that it might be some little inducement to him to come there himself. The compliment, however, at the time, was not so very flattering. For so forlorn and unimposing was this little out-of-the-way settlement, that our fathers, who delighted in puns, anagrams, alliterations, and other modes of playing upon words, used rather familiarly to call it *Lost-town*. Let them be excused, if, by such pleasantries, they sometimes sought to alleviate the discomforts of their lot. The place soon began to wear a more cheering aspect, and flourished more and more, until it far exceeded in importance the parent-town whose name it inherited. Our elder writers ascribe much of its early prosperity to the wisdom, conduct, and credit of Mr. Cotton, who seems to have had something of the talent of the Athenian statesman, who, when laughed at because he had no skill to touch the lute, retorted that he knew not how to fiddle; but he knew how to raise a small city into a powerful state. In New England, "a little one became a thousand, a small one a strong nation."

Arrival at Boston

Just before his arrival, the people had been holding a special season of fasting and prayer, urging their covenant with God as a reason why he should send them a spiritual guide, to be unto them, like Hobab to the tribes of Israel, "as eyes in the wilderness." Their supplications were answered in the gift of this "able minister of the New Testament." Mr. Cotton was then about forty-eight years of age, and ripe in wisdom, knowledge, experience and grace. At his coming, his services were called for in different directions. His great capacities for usefulness were considered to be the common property of the whole colony, and it was at first proposed that his support should be provided for from the colonial treasury, in consideration of the public benefit expected to accrue from his labors. However, this motion was very properly overruled. The magistrates and other leading men decided that this great light must be set in the chief candlestick, and, within a fortnight, designated him to be Teacher of the First Church in Boston, of which the Rev. John Wilson was then Pastor.

Admission to the Church

Mr. Cotton was first to be admitted to the church. This was an interesting scene. There was a stated religious service held on the Saturday evenings. At the first of these meetings after his landing, he, by request, took part in the discussion of the question, which, on that occasion, happened to be in reference to the church. He expatiated upon the diversities in the spiritual state and grades of purity of different churches. He showed from the Song of Solomon 6:8, that some churches are as queens, some as concubines, and some as virgins. After this, he and his wife were propounded for admission.

On the Lord's Day following, he conducted the exercises of public worship in the afternoon. He then expressed his desire to make a confession of his faith, according to usage. His confession related chiefly to the subject of baptism, which he then desired for his child. He gave his reasons for not baptizing it while at sea, from which it appears that he then held that the sacraments can only be administered in a settled congregation, or organized church; and also, that a minister, notwithstanding his official character, can dispense the seals only in his own congregation. On this last point, at least, he afterwards changed his views so far as to maintain that a minister might give the sacraments in a church which is destitute of the proper officers.

Mr. Cotton next requested the admission of his wife, to whose qualifications for membership he bore "a modest testimony." He craved that she might be excused from making a public oral profession of her faith, as was then the custom of the church. He regarded the practice as 'unfit for women's modesty,' and contrary to the apostle's rule. To her examination in private by the elders, he had no objections. So she was asked, whether she consented to the confession of faith made by her husband, and concurred in his desire for admission. Upon her answering in the affirmative, they were both admitted by vote of the church. Their child was then baptized by Mr. Wilson, the father himself presenting it. At the baptism of another child, which took place at the same time, he gave it as a reason for disusing the unscriptural and unnatural custom of employing sponsors, that the ordinance was designed as the "parents' incentive for the help of their faith."

Installation

A month afterwards, October 10, 1633, a day of fasting was observed. Thomas Leverett, "an ancient, sincere professor," an old parishioner of Mr. Cotton, and his fellow-voyager to this country, was chosen ruling elder; and Mr. Firmin, "a godly man," was elected deacon. These officers were ordained by imposition of the hands of the presbytery, that is to say, the pastor, and such ruling elders as were previously in office. The pastor and other officers of each particular church constituted the presbytery of that church, and in this sense alone can the term Presbyterian apply to our Congregational Churches.

This business being over, Mr. Cotton was then publicly chosen by the Church to be their Teacher, which was made manifest by the members' lifting up their hands. Next, the pastor, Wilson, demanded of him whether he accepted that call. After a pause, he replied to the effect, that he knew his unworthiness and insufficiency for the place; yet, recounting the particular passages of God's providence which concurred to call him to it, he felt himself constrained in duty to accept it. Upon this, the pastor and two ruling elders laid their hands upon his head, and the pastor prayed. Then, removing their hands, they again placed them on his head; and calling him by name, from thenceforth separated him to the said office in the name of the Holy Ghost, laid upon him the charge of the congregation, and in this significant manner indued him with all the privileges of his station. Last of all, they formally blessed him. The presbytery of the church having thus completed its part in this interesting ceremony, the ministers of the neighboring churches there present gave him, at the pastor's request, the right hand of fellowship. The pastor finally made a mutual stipulation between the church and its newly inducted teacher.

Laying on of Hands

In respect to the solemn imposition of hands, just spoken of, or ordination as it is often termed, we must observe that it does not follow of course, that Mr. Cotton renounced the ministry he had formerly received in the

Church of England. This may seem to be the natural supposition. But it must be borne in mind, that when, three years before, Mr. Wilson was constituted teacher of the same church, it was done in a similar manner; but with a *protestando*, that it was no re-ordination, as we now understand the term. These are the words of Governor Winthrop, who assisted on that occasion: "We used imposition of hands, *but with this protestation by all*, that it was only as a sign of election and confirmation, not of any intent that Mr. Wilson should renounce his ministry he received in England."[1] This is sufficiently explicit. And when the same Mr. Wilson, about one year prior to Mr. Cotton's arrival, was made pastor of the same church in which he had been thus constituted teacher, this too was done by the laying on of the hands of the ruling elder and the deacons. Of course, in this case, no protestation was needed, for it is impossible to suppose that the Church would nullify its own previous ordinance. Nor was any express protestation necessary in Mr. Cotton's case; for it had already been established, by the precedent in Mr. Wilson's instance, that no renunciation of his previous ministerial authority was intended.

The first installation in New England in which the laying on of hands was omitted, was that of Rev. Charles Morton, settled over the First Church in Charlestown, the 5th of November, 1686. Mr. Morton thus alludes to the subject in a letter written some three years after to the

---

[1] John Winthrop, *The History of New England*, 52.

right honorable Hugh Boscawen, Esq., in England: "Though their custom has been a new imposition of hands upon every new call to the exercise of the ministry, yet to us, who came from Europe, Mr. Bailey[2] and myself, it was abated. And for aught I can perceive, they mind more the substance of religion, than the circumstances oi some men's private opinions."[3] Dr. Increase Mather gave the charge, "and spoke in praise of the Congregational way, and said, were he as Mr. Morton, he would have hands laid on him." Rev. Joshua Moodey[4] also, in his prayer, alluded to the subject, and intimated that, "that which would have been grateful to many, namely, laying on of hands, was omitted."[5] From that time, the precedent set by Mr. Morton, in the case of resettling ministers who had been previously ordained, was followed more and more, until it became the constant practice. Previous to this change, ministers, in the intervals between one pastoral care and another, were regarded as they are now. They were spoken of, and treated as ministers, and exercised their function as occasion required. Reimposition, when used, was not intended to restore the ministerial

---

[2] Installed October 6, 1686, in Watertown, Massachusetts; afterwards pastor of the First Church in Boston.

[3] This letter is transcribed in part into a very admirable work by Samuel Mather, D.D., called *An Apology for the Liberties of the Churches in New England* (Boston, 1738), 148.

[4] Pastor for the First Church in Boston.

[5] William Ives Budington, *The History of the First Church in Charlestown*.

character, as though that had been lost; but to designate the person to a special charge.

Our fathers neither regarded imposition of hands as an act that could not be repeated, nor as essential to the validity of an ordination. Theodore Beza, Calvin's famous successor at Geneva, never received it, and under John Knox's influence, it was for some time disused in Scotland. It was not an act that could not be repeated. They viewed it simply as a solemn designation of the individual to a particular office or duty in the church, and as a sign of investiture. They held that every true minister must, in the first place, be inwardly called to the work by the Spirit of God, as Aaron was; and then he must be outwardly called by some church of Christ. They held that this power of external vocation, which belongs to the church, is far superior to ordination, which, indeed, is included in it, as the less is included in the greater. The church being able to give a lawful calling to a minister is much more able to carry that call into effect by the simple ceremony used for that purpose by the brethren in the apostles' time. Hence they maintained the validity of what is sometimes called lay-ordination, but which they, regarding it as the act of the whole body of the church, the original source of all spiritual power, considered as having in it more of ecclesiastical authority than if performed only by some of its officers acting by delegated powers. Accordingly, in some very few instances, the ceremony was performed, even in the presence of numerous ministers, only by the presbytery, or officers of the particular church, occasionally assisted by some of the brethren. This was done merely by way of asserting and establishing the great principle that the power of ordination resides in, and emanates from, the Church. After this had been sufficiently understood, it became the invariable custom, and so continues to this day, that the ceremony should he performed by other ministers. But though administered by councils, it is still regarded as done solely at the request of the church which convenes the council for that purpose.

Distinction between Offices of Pastor & Teacher

The distinction between the duties of the pastor and teacher is thus defined in the Cambridge Platform: "The pastor's special work is to attend to exhortation, and therein to administer a word of wisdom; the teacher is to attend to doctrine, and therein to administer a word of knowledge." Both are empowered to dispense the sacraments, to execute church-censures, and to preach the Word, as to which duties, "they are alike charged withal." The pastor, on whom chiefly devolved the care of the flock when out of the pulpit, was expected to spend his strength mostly in exhortation, persuading and rousing the church to a wise diligence in the Christian calling. The teacher was to indoctrinate the church, and labor to increase the amount of religious knowledge. His workshop was the study, while the pastor toiled in the open field. Thus Mr. Cotton gave himself up to reading and preparation for the instruction of his people. Twelve hours of close application he used to call "a student's day," and such a day's work he usually performed, secluded among his books. For intelligence respecting the state of his flock, he depended mostly upon the pastor and ruling-elders. He received many visits, but seldom made any himself. Perhaps it may help to a clearer understanding of the difference in the nature of these two offices, to state, that when a case of excommunication occurred, it belonged to the pastor to conduct the business and pronounce the sentence, if the offense related to immorality or "disorderly walking," but if it were a matter of heretical or erroneous opinions, it was expected that the teacher would preside.

In the estimation of our fathers, the pastor's station was considered to have rather the priority in importance and dignity. It has been a source of perplexity with some, how this could be, seeing that the teacher was sometimes much more distinguished, as to his attainments and general character than his colleague, as happened in this case of Mr. Cotton as compared with Mr. Wilson. But it seems to be very intelligible that a man may be pre-eminently endowed with the qualifications needful in a religious teacher, and yet be comparatively unfit for the more active duties of the parochial care. On the other hand, a man may be admirably fitted to *watch* as a pastor over the flock of God, who is comparatively disqualified to *feed* that flock with knowledge and understanding.

It must not be supposed that our fathers instituted two orders in the ministry. They firmly held, that all ordained ministers were of equal rank, and that there is not the slightest superiority of one over another, except such as results from superior wisdom, knowledge, piety, zeal, and reputation arising from either or all of these, by which individuals are occasionally elevated to a higher degree of estimation and influence than their brethren generally. With them, the terms *elder*, *pastor* and *bishop*, were synonymous and interchangeable, as they are in the New Testament, where they are used as different names for the same office. The distinction between the duties of the pastor and teacher was merely a division of the labors belonging to their common calling, each taking the part for which he was best qualified, without considering whether, in personal matters, he were the greater or more honored of the two. The precedence was accorded to the pastor, because the part of the work assigned to him is essentially the more important part. For "the word of wisdom," in which he was to deal, must be considered as more honorable than "the word of knowledge," which was the allotted province of the other. Without any disparagement of the latter, we may assent to the poet's estimate of the relative value of each—

> Knowledge dwells,
>   In heads replete with thoughts of other men;
> Wisdom in minds attentive to their own.
>   Knowledge, a rude, unprofitable mass,
> The mere materials with which wisdom builds,
>   Till smoothed, and squared, and fitted to his place—
> Does but encumber what it seems to enrich.

Knowledge is proud, that he has learned so much;
Wisdom is humble, that he knows no more.[6]

In this matter we may give more weight to an opinion of Martin Luther's, recorded in his "Table Discourses," as it seems in some sort to be a decision against himself. "One asked Luther, 'Which were greater and better—to strive against the adversaries, or to admonish and lift up the weak?' He answered and said, 'Both are very good and necessary; but it is somewhat greater and better to comfort the faint-hearted.'"[7]

The usage which now prevails in our churches does not so much set aside the distinction between pastoral and teaching duties, as blend both offices in one person, who is both pastor and teacher to his congregation. Most of our churches think themselves too small to require the labors of two officers, and too poor to sustain them. It were well, if they generally took better care of the single minister in whom these duties are united. Indeed these duties naturally run into each other, and it is impossible precisely to point out their bound-marks. It is now expected that doctrine shall be preached practically, and that practice be preached doctrinally. It is expected that each shall be so discussed, as that one shall involve the other, and their mutual relations be distinctly exhibited.

---

[6] William Cowper (1731–1800), *The Winter Walk at Noon*, lines 38–41.

[7] Cited in Antonius Lauterbach, *The Familiar Discourses of Dr. Martin Luther* (London: Baldwin, Craddock, and Joy, 1818), 239.

Perhaps it would be well for larger and more affluent churches to restore the ancient usage, which our earlier churches practiced so far as they were able. It is very rare to find a person who combines the requisites of a pastor and a teacher in a high and equal degree. And the killing attempt to unite each sort of excellence, where nature had conferred but one, has often occasioned a lamented waste of life and talents. The distinction recognized by our fathers still exists, as it must in the nature of things. How often it is said, "Such a one is a fine preacher, but no pastor; and that another is a faithful and successful pastor, but does not excel so much in the pulpit." And their respective hearers, who have sense enough to know that they cannot have every kind of perfection in one man, try to be thankful for such as they have.

"God's Promise to His Plantation"

About this time Mr. Cotton preached a sermon, which has been repeatedly printed under the title, "God's Promise to His Plantation." Its object is to exhibit the reasons which may justify so serious a step as the forming of a new settlement, like that in which he and his associates were engaged. Its chief felicity, however, is the text, "Moreover I will appoint a place for my people Israel, and I will plant them, that they may dwell in a place of their own, and move no more."[8] Whatever fastidious critics

---

[8] 2 Samuel 7:10.

may think of our forefathers' antiquated sermons, it cannot be denied that they had a singularly happy faculty of finding appropriate texts for every occasion. Mr. Cotton's selection, in the instance now referred to, had the additional merit of being fulfilled in the result. In our fathers and their posterity, was fulfilled that which was spoken by the prophet of the Lord: "He hath cast the lot for them, and his hand hath divided it unto them by line; they shall possess it forever, from generation to generation shall they dwell therein. The wilderness and the solitary place shall be glad for them; and the desert shall rejoice, and blossom as the rose. It shall blossom abundantly and rejoice, even with joy and singing."[9]

Ecclesiastical & Civil Affairs

At the time of Mr. Cotton's arrival, the ecclesiastical and civil affairs of the colony were in a confused plight. Under his advice, the state of affairs improved so rapidly, and became so well arranged, as to give some countenance to the expression of one by no means friendly to what he calls "the innovating genius of the great Cotton," and who speaks of him as "sovereign in his dogmas, and absolute in power." One of our oldest historians has said, "Such was the authority he had in the hearts of the people, that whatever he delivered in the pulpit was soon put into an

---

[9] Isaiah 34:17.

order of court, if of a civil, or set up as a practice in the church, if of an ecclesiastical concernment."[10]

Our Congregational churches are greatly indebted to him for that pre-eminent liberty they enjoy. The liberty and power which Christ the King had vested in his people, had for ages been wrested away by men who, like all usurpers, proved to be tyrants, and turned, as the Puritans said, "the Lord's house into a house of Lords," where they domineered over the faith and consciences of the disciples. The rightful power and freedom of the churches was, by Mr. Cotton, deduced afresh from the Scriptures, and fully re-established in practice. Our churches have ever since been nobly jealous and tenacious of that *free ecclesiastical order* which Christ conferred upon them, and for whose restoration they are indebted, under God, to Mr. Cotton and his pious and learned associates.

An eccentric preacher of the Wesleyan persuasion, who has been for some time deceased, is said to have publicly characterized the most numerous denominations in New England in this manner: "The watchword of the Congregationalists is, order! order! That of the Baptists is, Water! water! And that of the Methodists is, Fire! fire!" We have good reason to be satisfied with our part of this description. For water and fire are good servants, but very bad masters; or as the Duke of Bridgewater was wont to say, "They are the best of friends, but the worst

---

[10] William Hubbard, *A General History of New England* (Cambridge: Hilliard & Metcalf, 1815), 182.

of enemies." On the other hand, "order is heaven's first law." It is this which makes all the difference between the stately walls of the temple, and heaps of stones and building lumber. Ben Johnson sententiously observes: "It is only the disease of the unskillful, to think rude things greater than polished, or scattered more numerous than composed." And Dryden's rhyme affords us a valuable precept—

> Set all things in their own peculiar place;
> And know that order is the greatest grace.[11]

Richard Hooker rejoiced, on his death-bed, at the prospect of soon entering a world of order. And doubtless the church on earth will more closely resemble the church in heaven, when every minister and every member shall be, as godly John Norton says Mr. Cotton was, "like the heavenly bodies, always in motion; but still careful to keep within his proper sphere."[12] The God whom we worship and serve, "is not the author of confusion, but of peace, as in all churches of the saints."

Keys of the Kingdom of Heaven

Their first printed guide in ecclesiastical matters was John Cotton's celebrated book, entitled, *The Keyes of the*

---

[11] John Dryden (1631-1700), cited in *Encyclopaedia Londinensis*, vol. 8 (London: J. White, 1810), 756.
[12] Norton, *Memoir*, 53.

Kingdom of Heaven. This work has been recently republished by one of our enterprising booksellers; and a treatise so curious and instructive ought to have a wide circulation. It is chiefly interesting as a demonstration, that every individual church, with its own officers, is the depository of "the power of the keys." In other words, all the ecclesiastical rights and powers which Christ has given to his Church, are given to every regularly constituted independent church.

In describing the metes and bounds of church power, Mr. Cotton argues that, as in the State, there is a division of powers into several hands, which are to concur in all acts of common concern, and which arrangement results in a healthy constitution of the body politic. This book maintains that a church, duly organized with its own proper officers, has within itself all that is necessary to its continuance and well-being, and to the management of its own elections, admissions, and censures. Elders and brethren are the constituent members of this sacred corporation. The elders are entrusted with government, the brethren are invested with privilege. The church is so to be ruled by its elders who are over it in the Lord, that without them nothing may ordinarily be done, and that they may have a negative upon the votes of the fraternity, and that they alone may authoritatively preach and administer sacraments—yet are the brethren to be so upheld in their liberties, that, *unless with their consent*, nothing of common concern may be imposed upon them. Because particular churches may abuse their power, the book of the keys asserts the need of church communion in synods or councils, which may determine, declare or enjoin such things as will correct abuses or disorders in the offending congregations. But still to such churches themselves must be left the *formal acts* which are requisite for carrying out the advice of the council. If such advice should be scandalously and obstinately refused, then it will be the duty of the council to *withdraw communion* from the contumacious church.

Soon after its publication, the famous Dr. Owen undertook to confute it; instead of which, quite contrary to his expectation, it confuted and converted him. While speaking of its effect upon his mind, he makes the following remark: "And, indeed, this way of impartial examining all things by the Word, comparing causes with causes, and things with things, laying aside all prejudicate respects unto persons, or present traditions, is a course that I would admonish all to beware of, who would avoid the danger of being made Independents."[13]

---

[13] John Owen, *A Review of the True Nature of Schism* (Oxford: T. Robinson, 1657).

5
Controversies

Difficulties in the Way of Our Forefathers

The enterprise in which our fathers were here engaged, when Mr. Cotton joined them, was one of great difficulty, as well as great importance. They had some general ideas derived from their sacred oracle—the Bible—of the nature of the free government in the Church and in the State, which they wished to set up. But they were sorely perplexed in trying to reduce those ideas into practical forms. It was a novel undertaking. They had no experience of other men to guide them. They were pioneers. They were to strike out a new path, through jungle and through forest, to reach the high and glorious results toward which they were looking. But, at the outset, they were themselves confused in the intricate and untraveled maze. They were at a loss to find the due bearings and proper starting points.

At this juncture Mr. Cotton came to their aid. To them he seemed like that other John, who was the Lord's herald: "the voice of one crying in the wilderness, 'Prepare ye the way of the Lord, make his paths straight.'"[1]

Relation between Church & State

He never attained to the great conclusion, to which the present age has come, that there ought to be an *entire* separation of Church and State. But he led the way to it by taking a position much nearer to it than that which was then occupied by the Christian world. He taught that the ecclesiastical power is totally distinct from the civil power; and that, though they be closely connected, they are never to be confounded. This distinction prepared the way for their separation. Mr. Cotton thus expressed himself on the subject.

"God's institutions, such as the government of church and commonwealth be, may be close and compact, and coordinate one to another, and yet not confounded. God hath so framed the state of church government and ordinances, that they may be compatible to any commonwealth, though never so much disordered in his frame. But yet when a commonwealth hath liberty to mould his own frame, I conceive the Scripture hath given full direction for the right ordering of the same, and yet in such sort as may best maintain the well-being of the church. Mr. Hooker doth often quote a saying out of Mr. Cartwright, though I have not read it in him, that no man fashioneth his house to his hangings, but his hangings to his house. It

---

[1] Mark 1:3.

is better that the commonwealth be fashioned to the setting forth of God's house, which is his church, than to accommodate the church frame to the civil state."[2]

In following out these sentiments, the colony, where "the commonwealth had that liberty to mould its own frame," could not fail to conform to the republicanism of the Congregational church polity in which our fathers believed.

Abstract of Mosaic Laws

As all the freemen of this new-born republic were church members, it was thought that the law of God ought to be their rule in civil affairs. The General Court desired Mr. Cotton to draw up an abstract of the laws of Moses, omitting such as were of temporary obligation, and in their nature peculiar to the Jewish polity. This service he performed, and the fruit of his labor was many years after printed at London by William Aspinwall in 1655. From this transaction some malicious joker has taken occasion to say, that our fathers voted that they would be governed by the laws of Moses, until they could find time to make better. The jester had personal reasons, no doubt, for disliking the Mosaic legislation, which is very severe upon slanderers and such as bear false witness. Mr. Davenport gives the following correct account of the matter:

---

[2] Hutchinson, *History of Massachusetts*, 437.

Considering that these plantations had liberty to mould their civil order into that form which they should find to be best for themselves, and that here the churches and commonwealth are complanted together in holy covenant and fellowship with God in Christ Jesus, he did, at the request of the General Court in the Bay, draw an abstract of the laws of judgment delivered from God by Moses to the commonwealth of Israel, so far forth as they are of *moral* that is, of perpetual and universal equity among all nations, especially such as these plantations are: wherein he advised that Theocracy, that is, God's government, might be established, as the best form of government, where the people that choose civil rulers are God's people in covenant with him.[3]

Mr. Cotton's abstract was not adopted. Another drawn upon the same general principles, but with numerous deviations, some of them important, obtained the preference. It was printed in London in 1641, and has been supposed to be the joint labor of Mr. Cotton and Sir Henry Vane.[4]

---

[3] From a manuscript life of John Cotton by Mr. Davenport, quoted in Hutchinson, *Original Papers*, 161.

[4] Reprinted in the Collections of Massachusetts Historical Society, 1st series, vol. 5, 171.

Codification of Laws

This was soon superseded by another body of laws of the same general character, but with a much better arrangement. It is remarkable that the statutory system which was eventually adopted, was a code of laws systematically arranged under one hundred heads. It has been one of the chief commendations of the mighty mind of Napoleon that he was the first in modern times to apply the principles of plain practical common sense to the subject of legislation. That great man anticipated that "his fame in the eyes of posterity would rest even more on the code which bore his name, than on all the victories he had won." It has become the basis of the legislation of half of Europe. Within a few years the same method has been adopted in several of our States, and it has resulted in that recent revision of the statutes of Massachusetts, by which a chaos of laws was reduced to order and consistency. It is wonderful to find that this last great improvement, the codification of laws, was discovered and put in practice in this colony more than two centuries ago, and our learned modern citizens have, unawares, reverted to the method of their fathers. The honor of this boast of legislation belongs to the Rev. Nathaniel Ward, the witty and pious minister of the ancient town of Ipswich; and also a student of the science of law.[5]

---

[5] Ward's Code is reprinted in the Collections of Massachusetts Historical Society, 3rd series, vol. 7.

Mr. Cotton advised the people to persevere in their design of setting up a Theocracy, or divine government over a Christian commonwealth. His plan was to have the public affairs administered agreeably to the principles and requirements of revealed religion by executive officers appointed by the free election of the people. The people were to choose their own governors and other magistrates, and these officers were to govern themselves by the instructions of the Word of God. God, speaking by his Word, was to be owned as Chief Lawgiver and Supreme Head of their community. They who are disposed to laugh when they see the legal enactments of our ancestors backed up with texts of Scripture may as well save half a smile for Lord Bacon, and other of the highest judicial functionaries of England who, in those times, often confirmed their decisions in the same manner. Whoever will turn over the older parliamentary debates will find the haughtiest cavaliers in the House of Commons, triumphantly clinching an argument by appealing to Holy Writ. And doubtless when the prophecies are more completely fulfilled in the coming of the kingdom of God on earth, the day will come round again when it will be deemed meet for Christian people to regulate their political affairs by scriptural principles.

Relation between the Ministers & the Magistrates
As one result of this attempt in our colony, the ministry was brought into a very close alliance with the magistracy. For both the ministry and the magistracy, the people

cherished a religious veneration. Nor were they jealous of the intimate relations of their temporal and spiritual rulers, so long as the keys of power remained in the hands of the people by means of the elective franchise, both in Church and Commonwealth. Whenever any disposition to engross undue authority was betrayed, the people, notwithstanding their profound respect for their leaders, always promptly applied the never-failing remedy.

Good Mr. Norton says, "It was a usual thing, henceforth, for the Magistrate to consult with the ministers in hard cases, especially in matters of the Lord; yet so, as notwithstanding occasional conjunction, religious care was had of avoiding confusion of counsels: Moses and Aaron rejoiced, and kissed one another in the mount of God."[6]

John Cotton's Sermon

As an illustration of this matter, we may refer to an affair which took place in September, 1634. Mr. Hooker and many of his friends, who had at first settled in Newtown, were anxious to remove to Connecticut. Much opposition was made to their removal, and the two coordinate branches of the General Court came into very serious collision. Neither branch would yield to the other. In this painful emergency the whole Court appointed a day of fasting and humiliation, which was observed in all the

---

[6] Norton, *Memoir*, 47.

congregations. A few days after, the Court met again. Before proceeding to business, Mr. Cotton preached from Haggai 2:4: "Yet now be strong, O Zerubbabel, saith the Lord; and be strong, Joshua son of Josedech the high priest; and be strong, all ye people of the land, saith the Lord, and work; for I am with you, saith the Lord of hosts."

In his sermon the preacher severally described the strength of the magistracy, ministry, and people. Thus the strength of Zerubbabel, or the magistrate, is his official power and authority; the strength of Joshua, or the minister, is the purity of his life and teaching; and the strength of the people is their liberty. The preacher went on to show that, in matters of common concern, each of these three estates in the first instance, had a negative voice upon the doings of the others; and yet that the ultimate resolution ought to be in the whole body of the people. The sermon closed with an answer to all objections, and a solemn declaration of the people's right and duty to maintain their true liberties against any unjust violence or aggression. This discourse gave extraordinary satisfaction. All animosities and difficulties vanished, the various conflicting interests were reconciled, and all hands went to work vigorously, unanimously and peacefully from that day. Alluding to this affair, the reverend historian, Hubbard, says, "Mr. Cotton had such an insinuating and melting way in his preaching that he would usually carry his very adversary captive after the triumphant chariot of his rhetoric."[7] It was in accordance with the views expressed in that "political sermon," that he said on another occasion, "Purity preserved in the church, will preserve well-ordered liberty in the people; and both of them establish well-balanced authority in the magistrates. God is the author of all these three."[8]

It was another effect of his all-subduing persuasiveness that certain men of distinction who, in the heat of the recent controversy, had spoken disrespectfully to some of the magistrates, "being reproved for the same in open court, did gravely and humbly acknowledge their fault."

First Association of Ministers

The first association in Massachusetts was formed by the ministers of Boston and the vicinity about the year 1635. It met once in two weeks at the houses of the members. The usual business was the discussion of some important theological question. This association was regarded by some with a godly jealousy, lest it might, at a future day, encroach on the liberties of the people. The experience of more than two centuries has proved that this was a needless jealousy. The associations of Massachusetts, both local and general, have been highly useful and influential. At the same time, the independence of the churches has suffered no infringement.

---

[7] Hubbard, *History of New England,* 175.
[8] John Cotton, Letter to Lord Say and Seal.

Mode of Supporting the Ministry

Mr. Cotton's disposition to popularize the whole administration of religious affairs showed itself in the manner in which he chose to receive his salary. He insisted that it should be derived from the free-will offerings of the people. Once each Lord's Day, at the close of public worship, every member of the congregation who felt disposed to contribute to the support of the gospel, walked up to the elders' seat, where one of the deacons received the offerings. The proceeds were deposited in a public chest, out of which Mr. Wilson and his colleague received for their support one hundred pounds per annum. Considering how much greater was the value of money in those days, none of our ministers are now more amply maintained. The grace of God was bestowed on the First Church of Boston, even as, of old, on the churches of Macedonia; so that, "in a great trial of affliction, the abundance of their joy and their deep poverty abounded unto the riches of their liberality."[9]

Nor were the pastors, on their part, less disinterested. Not to speak of the proverbial generosity of that whole-souled man, Mr. Wilson, we find that, when subscriptions were made for charitable purposes, Mr. Cotton's donation would equal that of the wealthiest of his flock. In effecting his settlement here, he incurred expenses amounting to eighty pounds, which, at that period, was a pretty round sum. But when the people wished to

---

[9] 2 Corinthians 8:2.

reimburse it, he declined the offer, as not being necessary in his circumstances.

Indeed there is no trait more admirable in our fathers than their wonderful public spirit, and the readiness of individuals to make personal sacrifices for the general good. When people elsewhere marvel at the public and private munificence of the citizens of Boston toward all objects of literary, philanthropic and religious interest, we can say that they came honestly by this ennobling disposition, for they derived it in its full strength from their Calvinistic progenitors.

Most of the colonists who were men of property greatly impaired their estates by the sacrifices they made for the common cause. They were ever prompt to extend to each other a helping hand. Thus, when Governor Winthrop, neglecting his own affairs in his diligent service of the public, met with severe losses, the people spontaneously presented him with five hundred pounds.

The early part of Mr. Cotton's ministry here was disturbed by some violent storms of controversy. After these tempests had "wrought themselves to rest," there followed many calm and peaceful years.

Roger Williams Banished

In 1635, Roger Williams was banished from the colony. The merits of this controversy have been discussed elsewhere.[10] However, let it here be said, and that with all respect for the memory and character of that "fiery Welchman," that the action of our fathers in this matter is capable of a good defense, and that the condemnation they have generally received has been excessive and unjust. The matter is now mentioned merely with reference to Mr. Cotton's share in the transactions.

Controversy Between Him & Mr. Cotton

While the magistrates had the case of Mr. Williams under consideration, Mr. Cotton, with the neighboring ministers, whom the accused had once professed to hold in the highest veneration, presented a request that the civil authorities would stay their proceedings until the elders "had in a church-way endeavored his conviction and repentance." The ministers hoped that it was not from seditious principle that Mr. Williams had acted, but from a misguided conscience, which they expected to be able to set right. The magistrates acceded to the proposal of the ministers, but the governor, who too well understood the "nature of the creature," foretold to them, "You are deceived in the man, if you think he will condescend to learn

---

[10] In the original, McClure notes that the Roger Williams controversy is discussed in another chapter, but it is not exhaustive. For the scope of this book, the details of the controversy are only lightly touched upon.

of any of you." When other measures failed, and Mr. Williams was banished, Mr. Cotton wielded his pen in behalf of the magistrates. He published a letter concerning the power of the civil magistrate in matters of religion. The banished man replied to this letter, and also published a tract against the *Bloody Tenent of Persecution for the cause of conscience.* Mr. Cotton rejoined with another entitled, *The Bloody Tenent Washed and Made White in the Blood of the Lamb, being discussed and discharged of blood guiltiness by just defense, in answer to Mr. Williams; to which is added a reply to Mr. Williams' answer to Mr. Cotton's letter.* His opponent retorted with a treatise styled, *The Bloody Tenent yet more bloody by Mr. Cotton's endeavor to wash it white in the Blood of the Lamb, &c.* Here the dispute ended, as is usual in such cases, each party satisfied that he had the best of the argument.

Revival of Religion in First Church

For three or four years in the beginning of Mr. Cotton's ministry, the internal prosperity of his church was unexampled, and would, at this day, be regarded as a powerful *revival.* There were more conversions and admissions than in all the other churches of the colony. Many persons of profane and dissolute lives were surprisingly reformed and received into the bosom of the church. The discipline, admirably administered under the pastor Wilson and the ruling elder Leveret, was of singular benefit to the congregation. There were many "gifted brethren" into whose lips the Spirit of grace was poured, to the great edification and profit of the whole body of which they were members, which was in danger of being "exalted above measure through the abundance of the revelations."

Church Discipline

But clouds of thick darkness soon overcast the sunny prospect, and poured down their torrents, accompanied with the withering flash and the terrifying thunder. All at once the field, which was waving with such goodly harvest, was found to be sown with tares. Noxious weeds crept into that well-watered garden of gracious plants, and "roots of bitterness springing up troubled them, and thereby many were defiled."

Anne Hutchinson & the Antinomian Controversy

The prominent instigator of this mischief was a daughter of Eve named Anne Hutchinson. She was probably a pious woman, and certainly an artful one. On the ground of the apostle's direction that the elder women should teach the younger, she used to convene large numbers of females at her house, where she instilled into them the doctrines of antinomianism in their most demoralizing form. That she was worthy of the heaviest *ecclesiastical* censures, no competent judge of such matters can doubt. The justice of the civil disabilities under which she was eventually placed, must be considered elsewhere.

Her most active supporter was Rev. John Wheelwright, her brother-in-law, who preached as an assistant within the extensive bounds of the Boston church, which then included Braintree, where he principally labored. His partisans urged to have him associated as colleague with the other ministers, but Mr. Cotton evaded the connection on the ground that Mr. Wheelwright was an unsafe and violent man, and apt to raise questions of doubtful disputation.

Another of Mrs. Hutchinson's helpers was Sir Henry Vane, then a very young man, and newly arrived in the colony where, by his grave and dignified demeanor, he wonderfully took with the people, stealing their hearts, like Absalom, from their beloved Winthrop, whom he speedily supplanted in the chair of state. By his connection with the female heresiarch, he lost his popularity and his office, and soon returned to England. He there acted a very conspicuous part during the civil wars, resisted Cromwell's assumption of the protectorate, and was a staunch Genevan republican to the last. He died as a political martyr, being beheaded at fifty years of age for high treason against the ever-treacherous Stuarts. He is a striking instance of that late retribution by which posterity reverses the judgment of former times. The ablest literary arbiters of the present day proclaim this person, once so much abused, as one of the moral heroes of his eventful times, as a colossal champion of popular rights, and both as a civilian and theologian of vast and varied abilities. As a writer of prose in that age of great thinkers and authors, they announce him to be inferior only to the matchless Milton, and scarcely second even to him. That great poet has paid him a tribute sufficient to enrich his memory for many an age, in the following sonnet "to Sir HENRY VANE, the younger."

> Vane, young in years, *but in sage council old*,
>   Than whom a belter senator ne'er held
> The helm of Rome, when gowns, not arms, repelled
>   The fierce Epirot and the African bold;
> Whether to settle peace, or to unfold
>   The drift of hollow stales, hard to be spelled;
> Then to advise how War may, best upheld,
>   Move by her two main nerves, iron and gold,
> In all her equipage: *besides to know*
>   *Both spiritual power and civil, what each means,*
> *What severs each thou hast learned,* which few have done:
>   The bounds of *either* sword *to thee* we owe:
> Therefore on thy firm hand Religion leans
>   In peace, and reckons thee her eldest son.[11]

Upheld by these powerful supporters, Mrs. Hutchinson was enabled to raise a terrible commotion in the community. For a time, they had the address to procure the countenance of Mr. Cotton. This they did by giving him such explanations in private conversation as satisfied his unsuspicious nature of the orthodoxy of their

---

[11] Cited in John Forster, *Eminent British Statesmen* (London: Longman, Orme, Brown, Green, & Longmans, 1838), 147.

sentiments. Captivated by their ardent zeal and high professions, he gave heed to these "seducing spirits" for a time. But when, to his consternation, the vail of duplicity was thrown aside, he was shocked to find that he had unwittingly lent the sanction of his name to opinions so dangerous and corrupt. Upon this, the Antinomians charged him with dissembling, holding one set of opinions in the pulpit, and another in private discourse. This is the only transaction of Mr. Cotton's life which seems to have given serious offense to his brethren, who charged him with wavering and timidity.

His only fault, however, appears to have been the too great facility with which he suffered persons whom he had held in the highest estimation, to delude him as to their real sentiments, and to father their errors upon him. As soon as he was disabused, he exerted himself to repair the mischief. He publicly lamented his fault, in that he had slept in false security, while the enemy was sowing tares. In a letter to Mr. Davenport he says, "The truth is, the body of the island is bent to backsliding into error and delusions: the Lord pity and pardon them, and me also, who have been so slow to see their windings, and subtle contrivances, and insinuations in all their transactions."[12] Governor Winthrop gives this testimony of him that, "finding how he had been abused and made, as himself said, their stalking-horse (for they pretended to hold nothing but what Mr. Cotton held, and himself did think

---

[12] Norton, *Memoir*, 69.

the same), did spend most of his time, both publicly and privately to discover those errors, and to reduce such as were gone astray."[13] Among others reclaimed by his efforts was Robert Lenthal, the minister of Weymouth.

Long afterwards, on a general fast-day, "Mr. Cotton, in his exercise that day at Boston, did confess and bewail, as the churches, so his own security, sloth and credulity, whereupon so many and dangerous errors had gotten up and spread in the church; and went over all the particulars, and showed how he came to be deceived; (the errors being framed in words so near the truths which he had preached), and the falsehood of the maintainers of them, who usually would deny to him what they had delivered to others."[14] He was sufficiently humbled for a fault which appears to have been only the amiable infirmity of a heart too generous and confiding. When his eyes were opened to the duplicity which had been practiced, he spared no pains that he might rectify his mistake, and was very successful in arresting the spread of the evil. "By that means," says Hubbard, "did that reverend and worthy minister of the gospel recover his former splendor throughout the whole country of New England, with his wonted esteem and interest in the hearts of all his friends and acquaintance, so as his latter days were like the clear shining of the sun after rain."[15]

---

[13] Winthrop, *History*, 1:245.
[14] Winthrop, *History*, 1:253, 280.
[15] Hubbard, *History of New England*, 302.

Nearly the whole of the members of the church who resided within the present limits of Boston, favored the cause of Mrs. Hutchinson at the outset, with the exception of the pastor Mr. Wilson, Governor Winthrop and two or three others. This small minority had on its side all the ministers in the colony, except Mr. Wheelwright and Mr. Cotton, and nearly all the laymen of note. In this contest, so violent and almost unintelligible, it is surprising to see the same church, retaining as its ministers, those who were accounted the heads of the opposing parties. This fact, far more than any argument, evinces the prudence and Christian temper of the two men.

The principal errors of the Hutchinsonians were, first, the denial that sanctification is, in any sense whatever, an evidence of justification; and secondly, the assertion that the Holy Ghost dwells personally in every believer. Sir Henry Vane needed to go a little farther, and maintain that the Holy Ghost is united to the believer in the same manner as the divine nature is united with the man Christ Jesus.

The General Court took up the matter, though Rev. Hugh Peters sharply rebuked Governor Vane, and plainly hinted that if the civil authority would limit its action to "the things that are Caesar's," "the things that are God's" would go on much more quietly.

Mr. Cotton Implicated

The Court, having the matter under consideration, called for the opinion of the ministers. In the morning Mr. Cotton preached on the disputed points to general satisfaction. In the afternoon, Mr. Wilson made a lament over the dark and distracted condition of the churches, and the divisions occasioned by the newly broached opinions. At this speech Mr. Cotton, with Governor Vane and others, took deep offense and called upon the pastor to retract his expressions. Mr. Wilson, supported by the firm hand of Governor Winthrop, declined to give the satisfaction required. The contention threatened to wax sharp between them, but at last the wisdom and gentleness of the two ministers calmed the murmurings and mutterings which were ready to burst forth in a storm of strife. The next time Mr. Wilson preached, he was so happy as to give contentment to all.

As is usual in such cases, one error led on to another, heresy begat more heresy, and schism necessitated further schism. The ministers questioned Mr. Cotton on a variety of articles, and though most of his replies were satisfactory, others were not thought to be sufficiently explicit and unequivocal. Expressions and phrases were weighed and dissected with astonishing scrupulosity. Though Mr. Cotton was not to be shaken from his honest belief, yet neither was he betrayed into rashness.

A ship with passengers was about to sail for England. "Tell our transatlantic friends," said the teacher, "that all our strife is about magnifying the grace of God. Some seek to exalt the grace of God *towards* us; and some, the grace of God *within* us." Mr. Wilson, hurt at this, replied that he knew of neither elders nor brethren among their churches who did not labor to magnify the grace of God in respect to both justification and sanctification, or the grace of God both toward us and within us. As the people understood the matter of difference, the pastor, according to the nature of his office, naturally insisted on sanctification as "the grace of God within us," or gracious works, and experimental godliness. And the teacher, as the nature of his office might easily incline him, insisted more on justification as the free grace of God towards us pardoning us, not for our works or anything in us, but solely for the sake of Christ. Each of these worthy divines was full in the faith of both these points, but to either point a relative importance was assigned by one of the ministers beyond what the other would allow. Perhaps this unprofitable dispute was never better disposed of than by the excellent Rowland Hill, who once said in a sermon, "If I were asked which I loved the most, justification or sanctification, I would answer like the little children, when you ask them which they love best, father or mother? They will tell you, 'I love them both best.'"[16]

---

[16] Cited in William Jones, *Memoir of the Rev. Rowland Hill, M.A.* (London: Henry G. Bohn, 1845), 242.

Mr. Wheelwright Condemned

At their session in March 1637, Mr. Wheelwright was tried before the General Court for a highly inflammatory sermon preached on a fast day. He was adjudged to be guilty of sedition and contempt of Court, though Governor Vane and a few others entered their protest. There was a reluctance to proceed to the passing of sentence. The case was deferred to the next Court, and Mr. Wheelwright was recommended to the care of the Boston church, which had interposed a petition in his behalf. Meanwhile the discussions between the ministers had narrowed the ground of controversy until it was reduced to a mere hair-line of such fineness as to require the nicest sort of metaphysical eye-glasses to discern any room for further difference of opinion.

When the Court was again convened, Mr. Wheelwright confronted his judges with all possible boldness. He and his partisans had been so insolent and violent, as to injure their cause, but they were encouraged by some new arrivals which brought fresh strength to the antinomian standard. Their fanatical zeal blazed out in all directions with flaming extravagances which fired inflammable minds. Some were deranged with joys, and others with despair. The public excitement and distress was becoming intolerable. Days of fasting and prayer were observed with reference to the sad condition of affairs.

At a conference of ministers and elders held on the 30th of July, harmony was restored between Mr. Cotton and the other ministers: but Mr. Wheelwright, who was present, continued impracticable.

First Synod Held in New England

On the 30th of August, the first synod ever held in New England, was held at Cambridge. All the pastors, teachers, and elders in the country were present. They were boarded at the public charge, by which also was defrayed the traveling expenses of the members from the colony of Connecticut. This synod condemned eighty or more different errors, which had been set afloat in the community—Mr. Wheelwright remaining as pertinacious as ever. This condemnation was signed by all the members, except Mr. Cotton, who appears to have scrupled at the condemnation of two of the points specified.

Mr. Wheelwright Banished

On the 2nd of November the General Court assembled at Cambridge. After their long forbearance, finding all their attempts to reconcile Mr. Wheelwright unavailing, and feeling that a continuance of these dissensions absolutely endangered the existence of their little commonwealth, which was almost shaken to pieces thereby, they proceeded to banish him from their society. His sister, Mrs. Hutchinson, after a very singular trial of two days' duration, was also voted to be "unfit for their society," and required to leave it. Mr. Wheelwright went with many of his followers, and founded the town and church of Exeter,

New Hampshire. From thence he soon after removed to Wells in Maine; and after five or six years' absence, he owned his errors, made his retraction, and was restored to a residence in Massachusetts.

Mrs. Hutchinson Is Excommunicated & Banished

The unhappy woman who had fomented such a disturbance, after a short imprisonment, was set at liberty. But returning to her old course of agitation, she was summoned before the whole congregation on a lecture day, when her errors were enumerated and condemned, and a solemn admonition was read to her by Mr. Cotton, who decidedly reproved the disposition of the woman who had once been his most ardent admirer.

She then resided a while in Mr. Cotton's family, where he and Mr. Davenport labored to convince her, and bring her to repent of her errors. They so far prevailed with her, that she made a written recantation of most of her antinomian heresies, but in language so equivocal, as failed to satisfy the church. In an oral explanation she made a general confession of her delusions, so humble and penitential that they began to hope that she was really about to be reclaimed. But the moment they began to touch upon particular points, she became as wild as ever, and involved herself in such contradictions as amazed and alienated the last of her supporters and advocates. All hope in her favor being now abandoned, a motion was made for her excommunication. The long-suffering church, feeling a lingering tenderness for their erring sister, and something of horror at the thought of passing that dread sentence, still hesitated to take the step. At last, the resolution was adopted, and the gangrened limb was stricken from the body.

Her Unhappy End
After lingering with her friends awhile, she departed to an island in Narragansett Bay, which her husband and others had purchased of the Indians. Here they were ever starting some monstrous or foolish notion—such as, that women have no souls, that morality is antichrist, and that the devil and the Holy Ghost had an indwelling with every believer. Her husband dying about six years after, she again removed into the limits of the Dutch colony beyond New Haven. Here, in the following year, she came to the end of her earthly sorrows under the Mohawk scalping-knife. She perished with all her family of sixteen persons, except that one daughter was carried into captivity.

Writing Against Mr. Barnard & Mr. Ball of England
This protracted controversy being thus ended, Mr. Cotton found leisure to write a reply to a treatise which a Mr. Barnard in England had published against the mode of gathering the churches in this country. Mr. Cotton, in this year 1638, also replied to a defense of liturgies by Mr. Ball.

Thus this faithful soldier of the cross, ever valiant for the truth, had scarce panted through the toils of one sharp conflict, before he girded himself for fresh encounters. And, doubtless, it was no small relief, to turn from the struggle within the camp to meet an adversary abroad.

6
Legacy

Mr. Cotton's Success in the Ministry

After his troubles in connection with Mrs. Hutchinson's disturbances, which so afflicted him that he seriously meditated a retreat from the colony, Mr. Cotton passed the rest of his days in peace and high esteem. His labors in the pulpit and elsewhere were exceedingly great, and the power of God mightily attended them, and crowned them to the conversion of numerous souls, and the edification of thousands. Under the wise counsels of the noble and devout Winthrop in the State, and those of Mr. Cotton in the Church, the community prospered to such a degree, as to make the grateful inhabitants apply to them the words of the Psalm, "Thou leddest thy people like a flock by the hand of Moses and Aaron."[1]

Mr. Cotton knew how to touch the keys of the human heart, so as to draw out responsive and accordant notes. He played this complicated organ with a master's hand, and though he found it sometimes sadly out of tune, his

---

[1] Psalm 77:20.

skill would often blend the jarring sounds in surprising harmony. The church which he governed, with one or two exceptions, so peacefully, was organized of very discordant materials. Many of the members were strongly inclined to most of the forms of the national Church of England, in which they had been bred, and others were speculative and adventurous reformers who scarce knew how to be subject to any settled rule. But the patient sagacity of their teacher was marvelously successful in training them to habits of agreement and order.

Influence in the Community

A few instances are recorded which may serve to show the extent of his influence. In 1634, the people of Boston chose a committee for the division and distribution of the town lands, and purposely omitted to place any of the magistrates on the committee. Mr. Cotton soon persuaded them that it was more according to order, to refer such affairs to the civil elders of their Israel. And so they unanimously agreed to go into a new election, agreeably to his views.

In 1639, when the decays of their first rude place of worship, and the growth of the congregation, made it necessary to rear another, there arose a warm dispute as to the spot where it should stand. Their Teacher interfered with such success as to reconcile their opinions upon a point which, above all others, is apt to rend a congregation in sunder. The new edifice cost a thousand pounds, which this poor people cheerfully paid, without assessment, by voluntary contribution.

At an election held in 1641, it was proposed, that two of the deputies, who had fallen into low circumstances, should be dropped in favor of wealthier men. The Teacher, hearing of the project, generously but prudently condemned it at his next weekly lecture, in which he maintained that, if old and faithful officers had grown poor in the public service, instead of being discarded, they should be relieved at the public expense. The reproof was felt, and had its proper effect.

Women's Vails
In another case he proved that even the arbitrary fashions of female apparel could not withstand the weight of his solid counsels. Roger Williams and Mr. Skelton had persuaded the female part of their congregation at Salem that it was a religious duty for all women to wear vails in public worship. Mr. Cotton went there to preach on the Lord's Day. He was much struck at the oriental aspect of things in the congregation, so different from the customs of the English people, and in his forenoon instructions, he effectually took the vail from off the understandings of the ladies, and so enlightened their minds thereby that they all appeared in the afternoon without any vail upon their heads. And so that fashion passed away.

Independent Spirit of the People

But it would be the height of injustice to our free-spirited ancestors, to suppose that there was anything servile in the profound deference they usually paid to the suggestions of their civil and ecclesiastical leaders. When occasion required, they were not slow to show a stubborn independence with which it would not do to trifle. Thus in 1634, the people felt apprehensive that, by re-electing Winthrop, they should make way for a Governor for life. Mr. Cotton, then at the height of his popularity, in a sermon before the General Court, on whom the choice devolved, taught "that a magistrate ought not to be turned out without just cause, no more than a magistrate might turn out a private man from his freehold without trial."[2] No noise was raised about this dangerous doctrine, but at that same election, they turned out Winthrop, and put in Dudley.

Next year they ousted Dudley, and put in Haynes. The year after, they left off Haynes, and put in Vane. And all by way of practically showing their dissent from the doctrine that an elective magistrate has anything like a freehold tenure of his office. In 1639, the Governor and magistrate ventured to nominate three persons to fill vacancies in their board; leaving the people, however, as they said, "to use their liberties according to their con-

---

[2] *The North American Review*, vol. 44 (Boston: Otis, Broaders, & Co., 1837), 531.

sciences." And the people *did* use their liberties according to their consciences. They chose never a man of them. These were days, when "king Caucus" did not reign so despotically as now.

Such instances, rightly considered, are equally honorable to all the parties. It shows that the extreme deference ordinarily paid to their leading men, was not a blind and slavish submission, but a free and intelligent homage to their preeminent wisdom and worth.

Morality of the Colony

Such was the state of morals in those days that of twelve hundred men under arms on a training day, not one was intoxicated or guilty of profane language. Not long after this time, a sermon was preached in London before both houses of parliament, the Lord Mayor and Aldermen of London, and the Westminster Assembly of Divines, constituting the most remarkable auditory which the world could then have brought together. In that sermon, the preacher said, "I have lived in a country where in seven years I never saw a beggar, nor heard an oath, nor looked upon a drunkard."[3] That country was New England. In another place, additional testimony will be presented as to the high tone of morality in the first age of this country.

---

[3] Cited in Mather, *Magnalia*, 1:103.

Invited to Return to England in 1641

Mr. Cotton was by no means forgotten in his native country. The times were coming when "carousing cavaliers were turned to flight in every fight and skirmish," by "praying Puritans," those warriors of "iron grimness, stern as doom." It was about to be ascertained that solid "round-heads" were much too hard for empty "rattle-heads." The Long Parliament had begun to take matters in hand as parliaments had never done before. That persecuting power which had banished from Britain so many of the choice spirits of the land was now broken, and many of the wanderers were returning to their homes, while others were earnestly invited to avail themselves of the altered state of affairs. In 1641, a letter was addressed to Mr. Cotton and several other leading colonists, entreating them to return to the mother-country, and to take the part which would naturally fall to them, if there, in remodeling the institutions of the land. This letter was signed by the leading men in that great revolution including Oliver Cromwell. It was even in contemplation to send over a ship expressly for him.

Again Next Year to the Westminster Assembly

The next year, Mr. Cotton was invited with Mr. Hooker and Mr. Davenport to repair to England, and partake in the labors of the famous Assembly of Divines at Westminster. Mr. Cotton and Mr. Davenport were at first disposed to comply with the invitation, but were dissuaded by Mr. Hooker. The latter was decidedly opposed to the measure. He probably foresaw that the overwhelming preponderance of Presbyterian members in that Assembly would probably create great difficulty for any who were so fully committed in conscience and principle to the Congregational Way, as himself and his brethren here. There were in that Assembly five Congregationalists, commonly distinguished as the "Dissenting Brethren." These, with some help from about as many more of lesser note, kept the whole Assembly at bay for long years of debate and toil.

The great body of the members was deeply intent upon establishing a government by Presbyteries, Synods, and Assemblies, over all the churches of England without any toleration of other sects. They labored in this work with immense vigor, having all the power of the Long Parliament to back them. But do what they would, the invincible "Dissenting Brethren" had the amazing address to embarrass all their attempts. It was long before they could affect anything, except the preparation of the Catechisms, Confession of Faith, and such doctrinal articles in which they all agreed. And when at last, with extreme difficulty, the Assembly had completed their complicated model of church-government, and had begun to get a part of the machinery into actual operation, it was too late! All the wheels were broken at once, when Cromwell stamped with his heavy heel, and the Long Parliament vanished.

Congregationalists in the Assembly

Of that redoubtable "Five" were Dr. Goodwin and Philip Nye, who knew of old what a perilous debater Mr. Cotton could be. Right glad would they have been in those "wars of the Lord," to have had the aid of three champions from New England. But these latter were, doubtless, better employed in completing and settling the work in which they were here engaged. Mr. Hooker and Mr. Cotton were then occupied in the preparation of *A Survey of the Sum of Church-Discipline.* The first copy of this work was lost at sea by shipwreck on its way to England to be printed. Another copy had a happier passage, and was published at London in 1648. It is in two books, of which the first is by Mr. Hooker, and the other by Mr. Cotton. On the title-page first printed, the whole work is attributed to Mr. Hooker from which it has happened that Mr. Cotton's share in it has escaped the notice of most of those who have spoken of it. This was a very important treatise in its day, and it was edited and prefaced by Dr. Goodwin. The editor, alluding to the loss of the original copy, makes a remark upon it worth transcribing:

> The destiny which hath attended this book, hath visited my thoughts with an apprehension of something like an omen to the cause itself: that after the overwhelming of it with a flood of obloquies, and disadvantages, and misrepresentations, and injurious impressions cast out after it, it might in the time which

God alone hath put in his own power, be again emergent.[4]

He also compares the cause to seed-corn which, if it fall to the ground and die, together with some of those who scatter it, shall at last bring forth much fruit. These presages seem to be in latter stages of fulfillment. For though long depressed and, in a manner buried, the principles of Congregationalism have never, since the primitive ages, spread so rapidly as of late years.

Most of the ablest treatises which appeared in defense of those principles in the seventeenth century went from New England. Mr. Cotton did more in this way than any of our divines, but valuable books were prepared by Hooker, Davenport, Stone, Allen, Shepard, Richard Mather, Thompson, Welde, Norton, and others. This was the great controversy of their day. Our fathers studied it with care. There was scarcely a minister of note among them, who did not preach and publish upon it. They were far enough from setting the pattern for that spurious liberality, which is now so much in vogue, and which dreads to have anything said or done about Congregationalism for fear of making it sectarian.

---

[4] Thomas Hooker, *A Survey of the Sum of Church-Discipline* (London: Andrew Crook, 1658).

Synod of 1643

In the year 1643, all the ministers in the country, to the number of fifty, assembled at Cambridge. "They sat in the college, and had their diet there after the manner of scholars' commons, but somewhat better, yet so ordered as it came not to above sixpence the meal for a person."[5] This frugality is the most remarkable thing recorded of this synod. Mr. Cotton and Mr. Hooker were the moderators. The main business was to dissuade the Newbury ministers, Thomas Parker and James Noyes, from attempting to introduce the Presbyterian government in their church.

Synod of 1646–1648

While we are upon synods, we may as well speak of the most important meeting of the kind ever held in New England. It was convened at Cambridge late in 1646, under the auspices of the magistrates. After three sessions, the last of which terminated on the 28th of August 1648, they presented to the churches and the civil government, the celebrated "Cambridge Platform of Church Government." Having fully discussed the work, the General Court at its next meeting but one "thankfully accepted thereof, and declared their approbation of the said Platform of Discipline, as being, for the substance thereof,

---

[5] Cited in Winthrop, *History*, 2:165.

what they had hitherto practiced in their churches, and did believe to be according to the Word of God."[6]

Cambridge Platform

It thus received in Massachusetts the sanction of law, and indeed was adopted in all the New England colonies, Rhode Island excepted, until the Saybrook Platform was adopted in Connecticut sixty years after. I believe that the articles of faith in very many of our churches, expressly recognize the Cambridge Platform as presenting the principles of ecclesiastical order recognized and practiced by them. And yet if any one were to inquire how many, out of the thousands of members of those churches who have subscribed that declaration, have ever read the instrument referred to, the result would be, perhaps, more curious than gratifying. Less actual inconvenience, however, has resulted from the too general omission of the duty of examining this instrument than might have been expected. The principles of Congregationalism are so few, simple, and intelligible that the people obtain some general understanding of them without much special effort. Still *it would be far better* if the people who follow our system would read the book in which it is set forth, together with some of the valuable writings which have recently appeared on the same subject.

---

[6] *The Cambridge and Saybrook Platforms of Church Disciplines* (Boston: T. R. Marvin, 1829), 8.

But little now remains to be considered, except what relates to the personal character and habits of Mr. Cotton.

Mr. Cotton in the Family

In the family, he "ruled well his own house," as became one who so well "ruled his own spirit." If anything went amiss, he never corrected it in a passion, but with great deliberation, began by showing what precept of the Bible had been transgressed or disregarded.

At the devotions of the family, morning and evening, he read a chapter, explaining and applying the contents in a practical manner, but briefly. Before and after the reading, prayers were made, though very short and pertinent. He studied brevity in all, for he held "that it was a thing inconvenient many ways to be tedious in family duties."

The Sabbath he kept most conscientiously from evening to evening, and it is supposed to be from his example that the custom prevailed so extensively in New England of "resting according to the commandment" at the going down of Saturday's sun. When that evening arrived, he made a larger exposition at family prayer than at other times. Then the children and servants were thoroughly exercised in the catechism, probably using such as were of his own preparation, one of which called *Milk for Babes*, was used for feeding the minds of the New England children for many years after his death. Another called *Meat for Strong Men*, became their diet at a maturer age, "and nourished them up in the words of faith and of good doctrine." The catechising over, there followed prayer, and the singing of a psalm. Mr. Cotton then withdrew to his study, and its devotions, till the hour of repose.

The next morning, after the customary family worship, he retired to his private communion with God, until he went to the house of God, and its public duties. Returning to his home about noon, he at once secluded himself in his oratory or study, into which there must be no intrusion, except for the purpose of carrying him a very slight repast. At the time for afternoon worship, he came forth again, as one who had been holding converse with God in the mount of prayer. Coming back from the sanctuary, he first sought his retirement, and spent a season in closet prayer. He then prayed with his family, after which each one of the household repeated as much as could be remembered of the sermons of the day. In those days, this was the common practice in all Puritan families. Almost every person was provided with a book for the purpose of taking notes, so that the congregation looked, as we should say, like an assembly of reporters. This repetition of sermons was thoroughly attended to, and happy was the youth who could give the most exact account of text, *application*, *doctrine*, *divisions* and *uses*. Almost the only relic of this instructive custom, which has come down to our day, is the practice still preserved in some families of "bringing home the text." While the good old usage was kept up, the want of Sabbath schools for the religious instruction of the young was not much felt. Or rather, there was a Sabbath school, and that of the best kind in every family. In Mr. Cotton's household, when the repeating of the sermons was finished, with all the remarks and little explanations and discussions to which that exercise had given occasion, the evening meal was served up. After supper, another psalm was sung. Then the good man, lifting up his eyes and hands, would exclaim, "Blessed be God in Christ our Savior!"—and the Sabbath was done. Before retiring to rest, he again, in his study, committed all that he had done to that God whom he "served with a pure conscience."

Thomas Shepard

The sanctification of the Lord's Day was a very conspicuous trait of Puritan piety. Good Thomas Shepard gives as a reason for migrating to this country that he "saw the Lord departed from England when Mr. Hooker and Mr. Cotton were gone."[7] That excellent man was extremely scrupulous in observing God's holy day. His preparations for the pulpit were commonly finished by two o'clock on Saturday afternoon, in allusion to which he once used these words, "God will curse that man's labors that lumbers up and down in the world all the week, and then upon Saturday in the afternoon goes to his study, when as God knows that time were little enough to pray in and weep in, and get his heart into a frame fit for the approaching Sabbath."[8]

---

[7] Thomas Shepard (1605–1649).

[8] *The Works of Thomas Shepard*, vol. 3 (Boston: Doctrinal Tract and Book Society, 1853), 278.

Letter to Nathaniel Rogers

This bears rather hard on those ministers who are sometimes described as "Saturday-afternoon-men." Such, if any such there be, may derive instruction from the following extract from a letter of Mr. Cotton's, written to Rev. Nathaniel Rogers in 1630. "Studying for a sermon upon the Sabbath day, so far as it might be any wearisome labor to invention or memory, I covet, when I can, willingly to prevent it, and would rather attend unto the quickening of my heart and affections, in the meditation of what I am to deliver. My reason is, much reading, and invention, and repetition of things, to commit them to memory, is a weariness to the flesh and spirit too; whereas the Sabbath day doth rather invite unto a holy rest. But yet if *God's providence* have straitened my time in the week-days before, *by concurrence of other business not to be avoided*, I doubt not, but the Lord, who allowed the priests to employ their labor in killing their sacrifices on the Sabbath day, will allow us to labor in our callings on the Sabbath, to prepare our sacrifice for the people."[9]

Hospitality

Mr. Cotton was always noted for his hospitality. The stranger and the needy were entertained at his table with a pastoral benignity. It was rare that his house was without a guest. It was a gospel inn. He used to say, "If a man want

---

[9] See Sargent Bush, Jr. ed., *The Correspondence of John Cotton* (Chapel Hill: University of North Carolina Press, 2001), 156.

an heart for this charity, it is not fit such a man should be ordained a minister." While he lived in England, he was noted for his bounty to distressed ministers, many of whom were deprived by prelatical rigor of the means of subsistence before that rigor fell upon him. Many of the refugees who were driven from their flocks in Germany by the persecution then raging in the Palatinate of the Rhine, found a generous friend in him. Some of them were very eminent divines, who requited his kindness in Latin superlatives, the only coin the poor souls could spare. To his generous practice there is recorded one of those exceptions which "proves the rule." It shall be given in the words of Mr. Whiting, who is speaking of Mr. Cotton's manner of living at Old Boston in Old England: "His heart and doors were open to receive (as all that feared God so), especially godly ministers, which he most courteously entertained, and many other strangers besides. Only one minister, Mr. Hacket by name, which had got into the fellowship of famous Mr. Arthur Hildersham, with many other godly ministers, and being acquainted with their secrets, betrayed them into the prelate's hands, this man coming into Boston and meeting with Mr. Cotton, the good man had not the heart to speak to him, nor invite him to his house which, he said, he never did to any stranger that he knew of before, much less to any minister."[10]

---

[10] See Whiting in *Publications of the Narragansett Club*, 193.

Benevolence to Church of Segetea

Another instance in which Mr. Cotton showed himself to be one of those who "devise liberal things" occurred in 1651, while he was living in America. There was a little Congregational Church of exiled Puritans at Segetea in Bermuda, of which Mr. Nathaniel White was pastor. Banished by their opposers, this little flock retreated to one of the southern islands, a desolate spot where they suffered severe hardship. When the report reached Mr. Cotton, he exerted himself to procure collections for their relief. Near eight hundred pounds was contributed by some six or eight of the poor churches in the Bay. A fourth part of the sum was gathered by the Boston Church, where there was but one subscription that equaled, and none that exceeded Mr. Cotton's. The money was laid out in corn and other necessaries, and sent by the hand of two brethren in a small vessel hired for the purpose. It arrived at its destination, on the very day when the afflicted exiles had made a personal distribution of their last handful of meal, and had no prospect before them but that of speedily famishing to death. On that self-same day too, their believing pastor had preached upon that most suitable text, "The Lord is my Shepherd, I shall not want."[11] The admiring exiles could not sufficiently express their gratitude for this timely succor from their New England friends. "For the administration of this service not only supplied the want

---

[11] Psalm 23:1.

of the saints; but is abundant also by many thanksgivings to God."[12]

Learning

In reviewing what his contemporaries have said of Mr. Cotton, we cannot but be struck with the high repute in which he was held for learning. This was a quality in the absence of which no minister in the days of the Puritans could command respect. A pious and learned ministry, our fathers considered to be a necessary of life. A Dutch scholar of distinction heard Mr. Cotton preach at Boston in Old England and declared, "that never in his life had he seen such a conjunction of learning and plainness as there was in the preaching of this worthy man."[13] It was rare for him to allude to his own acquisitions, but in the confidence of friendship, Mr. Cotton once said, "That he knew not of any difficult place in all the whole Bible which he had not weighed somewhat unto satisfaction."[14] He had an immense library for those days, and an immense acquaintance with it. But his favorite author was one whose name is not apt to be spoken with commendation by "lips polite." Said Mr. Cotton, "I have read the fathers, and the schoolmen, and Calvin too, but I find that

---

[12] 2 Corinthians 9:12.

[13] Mather, *Magnalia*, 275.

[14] Cotton Mather quoted in William Buell Sprague, *Annals of the American Pulpit: Trinitarian Congregational* (New York: Robert Carter & Brothers, 1857), 29.

he that has Calvin has them all."¹⁵ When asked in his later days why he indulged himself in nocturnal studies more than formerly, he answered with a smile, "Because I love to sweeten my mouth with a piece of Calvin before I go to sleep."¹⁶ It is needless to ask what were the doctrinal sentiments of a man with such a moral taste as this. It is evident that he held to that Pauline system, which is properly the belief of minds naturally strong, or highly illuminated by the Spirit of grace. No person can be both an intelligent and ardent Calvinist, who has not either a profound and penetrating judgment, capable of grasping truths of the first magnitude, or else a heart intensely excited and irresistibly led by that spiritual influence, which the gospel describes as essential to salvation.

Habits of Study

The habits of Mr. Cotton, from youth to age, were those of an indefatigable student. He was an early riser, devoting the morning hours to closer application. In his later years, he abstained from any evening repast, occupying the time appropriated to supper in reading, reflection and prayer. Having a vigorous constitution, his life and labors were happily prolonged by careful diet and regular living. He rarely needed any other doctor for the body. Dryden says:

---

[15] Mather, *Magnalia*, 274.
[16] Mather, *Magnalia*, 250.

>   The first physicians by debauch were made;
>   Excess began, and sloth sustains the trade.[17]

He was "sparing of sleep, more sparing of words, but most sparing of time." His study was his paradise, which he never willingly left, except to do some good office. Unseasonable visitors, who consumed his precious time, he treated with all gentleness and urbanity, but after such a one had retired, he would say with some regret, "I had rather have given this man a handful of money than have been kept thus long out of my study." He kept by him a sand-glass which ran for four hours—this turned over three times measured his day's work. Of this no small part consisted in fervent prayer, for he held with Luther that he who has prayed well has studied well.

Manner of Preaching

In the manner of his preaching, Mr. Cotton was plain and perspicuous. He conscientiously forbore to make any display of his vast learning in the pulpit. He addressed himself to the common people. His chief anxiety was to be understood. He would often say, though apt to handle the deepest subjects, "I desire to speak so as to be understood by the meanest capacity." When an iron key would unlock the mystery of godliness better than a golden one, he preferred the cheaper, but more useful metal. The wish of

---

[17] John Dryden (1631–1700), *To My Honor'd Kinsman.*

Legacy

his heart was to glorify God rather than to win commendation for himself. At the end of all his manuscript discourses, he ever inserted this, or some similar phrase, "For thy glory, God!" In him, the fumes of the "odorous lamp" of science never dimmed the light of his piety.

He commonly bestowed great labor upon his public discourses, though he sometimes preached with very great effect when he had no preparation or warning. Sometimes, as he was going to the pulpit, his text would open to him in a new and striking manner; he would then unfold it by the hour, expressing himself with such steadiness and precision, that the most critical of his hearers would not be aware that they were listening to an unstudied effort.

In vindication of his plain and familiar way of preaching, Mr. Cotton would say, "If I preach more scholastically, then only the learned, and not the unlearned, can so understand as to profit by me; but if I preach plainly, then both the learned and unlearned will understand me, and so I shall profit all."[18]

He viewed the subject just as Martin Luther did, as he is reported to have expressed himself in his table talk. When Dr. Erasmus Albert was to preach before the prince-elector, Luther said to him, "Let all your preaching be in the most simple and plainest manner: look not to the prince, but to the plain, simple, gross and unlearned people; of which cloth the prince himself is also made. If

---

[18] Mather, *Magnalia*, 250.

I, in my preaching, should have regard to Philip Melanchthon, and other learned doctors, then should I work but little goodness. I preach in the simplest sort to the unskillful, and the same giveth content to all. Hebrew, Greek and Latin I spare, till we learned ones come together, as then we make it so curled and finical, that God himself wondereth at us."[19] At another time, the stout reformer exclaimed, "When preachers come to me, to Melanchthon, to doctor Pommern, &c., then let them show their cunning, how learned they be; they shall be well put to their trumps. But to sprinkle out Hebrew, Greek and Latin in their public sermons, the same savoreth merely of pride, which agreeth neither with time nor place, nor is it pertinent. In the church, among the congregation, we ought to speak, as we use at home in the house, the plain mother-tongue, which everyone understandeth, and is acquainted withal."[20]

Of the happy effect of Mr. Cotton's manner of preaching, we have a very pleasing and instructive example in the autobiography of that worthy old soldier of Jesus Christ, Captain Roger Clap. Having spoken of his admission to the Church in Dorchester, at its formation in 1630, he proceeds with the relation of his subsequent experience in religion. "Jesus Christ being clearly preached, and the way of coming to him by believing was plainly shown forth; yet because many, in their Relations, spoke

---

[19] Martin Luther, *Table Talk*.
[20] Martin Luther, *Table Talk*.

of their great terrors and deep sense of their lost condition, and I could not so find, as others did, the time when God wrought the work of conversion in my soul, nor in many respects the manner thereof; it caused in me much sadness of heart, and doubtings how it was with me, whether the work of grace were ever savingly wrought in my heart or no? How lo cast off all hope, to say, and verily to believe that there was no work of grace wrought by God in my heart, this I could not do; yet how to be in some measure assured thereof was my great concern. But hearing Mr. Cotton preach out of the Revelations, that Christ's Church did come out of great tribulation, he had such a passage as this in his sermon: "'*That a small running Stream was much better than a great Land Flood of Water, though the Flood maketh the greatest Noise: so,*' saith he, '*A little constant Stream of godly Sorrow, is better than great Horror.*' God spoke to me by it, it was no little support unto me. And God helped me to hang on that text (and through his grace I will continue so to do), namely, '*This is a faithful saying, and worthy of all acceptation, that Jesus Christ came into the world to save sinners.*'"[21] May the words of Mr. Cotton comfort some who read these pages, even as when they came with a blessing to that right old Puritan!

---

[21] Roger Clapp, *Memoirs of Capt. Roger Clap* (Boston: William Tileston Clapp, 1807), 10.

Controversial Writings

Besides his incessant preaching, and a large correspondence in which he was very usefully employed as a casuist, being expert in the solving of cases of conscience, he was much engaged in extraordinary labors. In the frequent fast-days appointed by his Church in those troublous times, he would be engaged in prayer and preaching for five and six hours together. He would also keep many whole days of fasting by himself, occupying the time with humiliation of his soul and prayer. He also observed, as occasion prompted, entire days of private thanksgiving for special mercies received.

Of all his more important publications, we have had occasion to speak in the course of this narrative. Most of them were called forth by the controversies which then agitated the Church on the subject of government and discipline. They are remarkable for the mild Christian spirit which pervades them. "None will blame a man," says Thomas Fuller, "for arming his hands with hard and rough gloves, who is to meddle with briers and brambles."[22] But though he had to deal with some of the most thorn-backed and scratching antagonists, they could not provoke him to anger. Though a most tenacious and vigorous maintainor of the truth, he never lost "the meekness and gentleness" which he learned of his divine Master. "It may fairly be said that an amiable spirit in controversy forms one of the most incontrovertible evidences of

---

[22] Fuller, *Holy and Profane State*, 52.

elevated piety, because it is precisely this point in which so many men of indubitable excellence have failed."[23] Good men have often debated, "as if personal invective, and embittering a style, were God's way of bettering a cause, or battering an opinion." As to the temper in which controversy should be conducted, Mr. Cotton may serve "as a pattern for all answerers to the world's end." Through the spirit in which he replied, he did like Job with the books of his adversaries, "and bound them as a crown to him."

Correspondence

We have alluded to his extensive correspondence. But little of it has escaped the ravages of time.[24] Among others, he maintained a friendly correspondence with Archbishop Usher. As a sample of the manner in which he wrote familiarly to his pious friends, an extract is here given from a letter dated the ninth of March, 1631; and addressed to the reverend Nathaniel Rogers, who was afflicted with a very tedious and disheartening malady. "I bless the Lord with you, who supporteth your feeble body to do him service, and meanwhile perfecteth the power of his grace in your weakness. You know who said it, 'Unmortified strength posteth hard to hell, but sanctified weakness creepeth fast to heaven.' Let not your spirit

---

[23] Jeremy Taylor, *The Whole Works*, vol. 1 (London: Frederick Westley and A.H. Davis, 1835), xlvi.

[24] See Sargent Bush, Jr., ed. *The Correspondence of John Cotton* (University of North Carolina Press, 2001).

faint, though your body do. Your soul is precious in God's sight; your hairs are numbered; and the number and measure of your fainting fits, and wearisome nights, are weighed and limited by his hand, who hath given you his Lord Jesus Christ, to take upon him your infirmities, and bear your sicknesses."[25]

Among other distinguished correspondents of Mr. Cotton's was one beyond comparison the greatest man of his time. The life of Oliver Cromwell is yet to be written. It has, as yet, been "attempted" only, and that in the most murderous manner. For a considerable period after his death, it would have been regarded as high treason to have presented a true picture of his merits. And when, at last, the expulsion of the Stuarts left historians at liberty to do some justice to Cromwell's character, the age had become too degenerate to understand or appreciate the man. The materials for his history were only such as had been collected by his bitter foes: whose only study was to conceal everything which could adorn his memory, and parade everything which could be found or invented to blacken it. The present generation takes its idea of the man, either from Clarendon, who hated his politics; or from Hume, who hated his religion; or from inferior authors, who hated everything about him. He is commonly regarded as a person of extraordinary talent, but whose talent lay chiefly in the line of canting hypocrisy. His fame, however, is destined to emerge from the clouds

---

[25] Sargent Bush, Jr., ed. *The Correspondence of John Cotton.*

which have so long obscured it. Whoever reads, with unprejudiced mind, the recent collection of his letters and speeches, wherein Cromwell speaks for himself in his own way, will feel a revolution in his opinions of the Protector. He possessed the very highest capacity for both military and civil affairs, ranking him among the very first of soldiers and statesmen. To this he added a piety the most profound and unaffected, constantly and naturally pervading all language, whether on the most private or public occasions. He assumed the high station which he so ably filled, in obedience to what he felt to be a divine call, requiring of him what he alone could have effected—the preservation of the peace, liberty and religion of his distracted country.

In Carlyle's collection we find the first of Cromwell's letters to Mr. Cotton, which was all written with the Protector's own hand. In connection with it, that strange "elucidator" remarks in his own fantastic idiom as follows, "Reverend John Cotton is a man still held in some remembrance among our New England friends. A painful preacher, oracular of high gospels to New England; who in his day was well seen to be connected with the Supreme Powers of this Universe, the word of him being as a live coal to the hearts of many."[26] Carlyle supposes that Cotton had been writing to Oliver concerning some act of Parliament for propagating the gospel in New England. This

---

[26] *The Collected Works of Thomas Carlyle*, vol. 11 (London: Chapman and Hall, 1869), 308.

is a mistake. The Protector had written to Rev. William Hooke, who was Mr. Davenport's colleague at New Haven; and who, a few years after, was one of Oliver's chaplains.

In his letter to Mr. Hooke, Oliver had sent loving and respectful salutations to Mr. Cotton. Mr. Hooke, whose wife was near of kin to Cromwell, intimated the message to Mr. Cotton, with the suggestion that a letter from him to the Protector would be taken in good part. Mr. Cotton accordingly wrote a letter of some length, which is preserved in Hutchinson's Collection. It is occupied, after the manner of a solution of a case of conscience, with a cautious vindication of Cromwell's policy, especially in the matters of dosing the Long Parliament with "Pride's purge," and demanding justice upon the head of a perjured and traitorous king. Mr. Cotton, having summed up the considerations belonging to the case in a manner accordant with the views which Cromwell himself appears to have taken of it, goes on to say, "These things are so clear to mine own apprehension, that I am fully satisfied, that you have all this while fought the Lord's battles, and the Lord hath owned you, and honored himself in you, in all your expeditions; which maketh my poor prayers the more serious, and faithful, and affectionate (as God helpeth) in your behalf."[27] This letter is dated the twenty-seventh of May, 1651. Cromwell's reply is dated the second of October following. It owns, as Carlyle says, "Their

---

[27] Oliver Cromwell, *Oliver Cromwell's Letters and Speeches.*

general relationship as Soldier of the gospel and Priest of the gospel, high brother and humble one; appointed, both of them, to fight for it to the death, each with such weapons as were given him."[28] Other letters, now lost, passed between them.

Personal Appearance

In stature, Mr. Cotton was rather low, and slightly inclined to be robust. He had a fair complexion, and ruddy countenance; and his locks, which were naturally brown, in his later life had a snowy whiteness, which, as "a crown of glory" made our patriarch's aspect venerable to behold. There was an inexpressible majesty in his mien, which compelled the respect of all who approached him, and the voice of profaneness was hushed when he was by. The inn-keeper at Derby, where Mr. Cotton often visited while he dwelt in England, used to tell his companions that he wished that man were out of his house, for he was not able to swear with him under his roof.

Pulpit Delivery

His voice was not strong, but clear and distinct, and heard with ease in the largest assemblies. He delivered himself in the pulpit with much dignity, using a natural and becoming gesture of the right hand. But such a divine power and holy unction attended his grave and earnest manner

---

[28] Oliver Cromwell, *Oliver Cromwell's Letters and Speeches*, Letter CXXV.

that Mr. Wilson said of him, "Mr. Cotton preaches with such authority, demonstration and life, that methinks, when he preaches out of any prophet or apostle, I hear not him; I hear that very prophet and apostle: yea, I hear the Lord Jesus Christ himself speaking in my heart."[29] O this is the true Christian eloquence, when the lips of the ambassador seem to breathe the very words of the Lord of life and salvation!

Equanimity

He had an almost miraculous evenness of temper. No insult could disturb his self-possession. Such was the meekness and mildness of his disposition that Mr. Norton used to regard him as the Moses and Melanchthon of the new world. In the words of that good old puritan, Simeon Ashe, "he was a dwarf in regard of humility, but a giant in regard of strength." Though but a lamb in his own cause, like his master, he was a lion in that of God and his church. His gentleness had nothing about it, either nerveless or cowardly. His chief services in behalf of the truth he loved were ever marked by a modest estimation of himself. "The highest flames," says Jeremy Taylor, "are the most tremulous; and so are the most holy and eminently religious persons more full of awfulness, and fear, and modesty, and humility."[30] Mr. Williams, when his adversary,

---

[29] John Norton in Mather, *Magnalia*, 275.
[30] Jeremy Taylor, *Works*, 72.

candidly owned the goodness of his heart, and commended his attachment to the truths of the gospel. Mr. Cotton once said to a confidential friend, "Angry men have an advantage above me; the people dare not set themselves against such men, because they know it will not be borne; but some care not what they say or do about me, because they know I will not be angry with them again."

Patience under Abuse

As a specimen of the manner in which he met abusive treatment, we are told that he was once followed from the church to his home by a peevish, complaining hearer, who tried to provoke him by telling him that his preaching had latterly become either very dark or very flat. To this he mildly answered, "Both, brother, it may be, both: let me have your prayers that it may be otherwise."[31]

On another occasion a very ordinary sort of a man had boasted of his clear insight into the book of Revelation. Mr. Cotton modestly replied, "Well, I must confess that I want light in those mysteries." Upon this, the man sent him by a servant a pound of candles. The good minister received this piece of impudence with a silent smile, revenging himself only by a Christian taciturnity. Mather,

---

[31] Mather, *Magnalia*, 252.

relating the circumstance in his maniloquent style, remarks, "Mr. Cotton would not set the beacon of his great soul on fire, at the landing of such a little cock-boat."[32]

The excellent Mr. Flavel relates an incident of this kind. While Mr. Cotton lived at Boston in old England, he was seen passing along the street by some gay young fellows, who had been at the tavern, indulging in that which Solomon says is a mocker; and is never more so than when it makes mockers of those who use it. One of them says to his companions, "I will go and put a trick upon old Cotton." Crossing over to the reverend and holy man, he whispered in his ear, "Cotton, thou art an old fool." That good man, without the slightest irritation, looked mildly at him, and replied, "I confess I am so: the Lord make both me and thee wiser than we are, even wise unto salvation." Returning abashed to his companions, the wanton insulter told them of this meek reply, which sobered for that time their intemperate mirth, and perhaps first taught them "how awful goodness is."[33]

These examples provoke a sort of impatience, that more of his expressions have not been preserved. We are sure that he daily uttered such instructive dictates of a mind, adorned with unaffected humility, singularly refined from the dross of earthly passions, and mellowed to a sweet maturity of grace by the ripening warmth of close communion with the Lamb of God.

---

[32] Mather, *Magnalia*, 283.
[33] Mather, *Magnalia*, 252.

Cause of Death

The labors of Mr. Cotton were hastening to a close by exposure to wet in passing the ferry to Cambridge, where he went to preach to the students. This sermon was from Isaiah 54:13: "And all of thy children shall be taught of the Lord." Among those who heard it was Increase Mather, then a young scholar, and in after life married to Mr. Cotton's only surviving daughter. Dr. Mather never forgot the impressions made upon his mind by that discourse. His powers of utterance failed while speaking. He was attacked with inflammation of the lungs, became asthmatic, and was seized by a complicated disease, which he felt as a warning that his end drew nigh.

Last Labors

The next Sabbath he took for his text the last four verses of the second epistle to Timothy, on which epistle he had been expounding in course. He told his auditory the reason of his taking so many verses at once, "Because else," said he, "I shall not live to make an end of this epistle." On the following Sabbath, being the twenty-fifth of November, he delivered his last sermon with much difficulty, on John 1:14, on the glory of Christ, "from the faith to the sight of which he was hastening." He had the feelings of another of the non-conforming divines, who said, "If I must be idle, I had rather be idle underground, than above ground." He chose rather to be dead, than live dead; having often expressed a wish that he "might not outlive his work."

Prepares to Die

This duty done, Mr. Cotton spent one day in his study, in special prayer and preparation for the last great conflict which he was assured was at hand. On leaving that beloved and familiar apartment, he remarked to his consort, "I shall go into that room no more!" He now betook himself to the couch, where he expected "the mercy-stroke of death," the blow that must shatter the last link with which sin or sorrow could fetter his soul. Although his foretastes and promises of heaven chiefly attracted him thitherward, he declared that it greatly contributed to his readiness to depart, when he considered the company of saints, so many of whom he had known and dearly loved, in whose communion he was shortly to mingle.

Closing Scene

Magistrates, clergymen, and private Christians in great numbers resorted to his sick-bed, mournfully listening to his dying counsels. Mr. Dunster, at that time President of Harvard College, with many tears besought his blessing, saying, "I know in my heart, they whom you bless shall be blessed." Shortly before his death, Mr. Cotton sent for the elders of the church, who prayed over him. He exhorted them to feed the flock of which they were overseers, and to watch against those declensions to which he saw that professors of religion were tending. He added, "I have now, through grace, been more than forty years a servant unto the Lord Jesus Christ, and have ever found him a good master." When his colleague, Mr. Wilson, a man who abounded in love as much as Mr. Cotton did in light, took his last leave, he breathed an ardent wish that God would lift up the light of his countenance upon the dying man; he promptly replied, "God hath done it already, brother!"

He then called for his children to whom he left the covenant of God as their chief portion. Having settled all his affairs, and taken leave of the world, he begged to be left alone for the little time he had to live, that his soul might be undisturbed in communing with his God. He caused the curtains to be drawn, and exacted a promise of the gentleman who attended him, that the privacy of his chamber should not be interrupted. Then reminding that gentleman, who was a beloved member of his church, of that promise, he gave him this parting benediction, "The God that made you, and bought you with a great price, redeem your body and soul unto himself!" These were the last words he was heard to utter. After a few speechless hours, he quietly breathed out his spirit into the hands of Him who gave it. This gentle translation of his soul from earth to heaven, took place shortly after eleven o'clock of Thursday morning, the twenty-third of December, 1652, in the sixty-eighth year of his age.

Funeral Obsequies

On the twenty-eighth of the same month, he was honorably interred by a mourning concourse of the people, among whom he had ministered in holy things for more than nineteen years. He was borne on the shoulders of his brother-ministers to his last sleeping place, in a tomb of brick, in what is called the "Chapel Burying Ground." A deep and sincere mourning was made for him by his afflicted flock, with whom all the scattered churches of New England joined their sorrows; and numerous elegies, according to the taste of the times, recorded the general grief. The lectures in his church during the following winter, preached, as they were by the neighboring clergymen, were but so many funeral discourses. In the first of them, by his old friend and fellow-laborer and fellow-sufferer, Richard Mather of Dorchester, he gave the following counsel to the church, "Let us pray that God would raise up some Eleazer to succeed this Aaron: but you can hardly expect that so large a portion of the Spirit of God should dwell in any one, as dwelt in this blessed man."[34] His departure was lamented as a public loss in all the churches of the country. In particular, Mr. Davenport most tenderly bewailed it in a sermon at New Haven, from the words, "I am distressed for thee, my brother, very pleasant hast thou been unto me."[35]

---

[34] Mather, *Magnalia*, 249.
[35] Mather, *Magnalia*, 249.

Dwelling-House

The south part of Mr. Cotton's dwelling-house was built by Sir Henry Vane, who boarded there with him until Sir Henry returned to England, first giving that addition to Seaborn Cotton. It stood on the lot south of what was lately the estate of Gardner Green, Esq. and was part of the ground now occupied by the "Tremont Row," nearly opposite to the Savings Bank. That rise of ground long bore the name of "Cotton's Hill." His house was still standing, then the oldest house in Boston, some twenty years ago.

Will

The inventory of his estate amounted to one thousand and thirty-four pounds, four shillings. His will provided that, in certain contingencies, half of his estate should go to Harvard College, and half to support the free school in Boston. Those contingencies never happened, but the provision made for them evinces his deep interest in the important work of education. To the Church he bequeathed a piece of silver plate to be used at the communion table, where at his first coming he had made use of wooden chalices. This reminds us of the lament uttered by one of the writers in the middle ages, who sighs for those days of primitive piety, when the church in her poverty had wooden cups, but golden priests: but now, alas! he cries, we have golden chalices and wooden priests.

Houses of Worship

The first place of worship in which he here officiated, and which was the first ever erected to God upon this peninsula, stood in what is in these republican days State street, but in those monarchal times was King's Street. It was built in 1632. There are lovers of liturgic pomp, who cannot feel the spirit of devotion unless awakened by columned aisles, and stained windows, and splendid altars, and sacred vestments, and responsive readings, and resounding organs, and choral chants. Such worshipers, as it has been forcibly said, "seem to have no idea of the Supreme Being but as a Grand Master of ceremonies to the whole universe." They would have scorned the adorations of that mud-walled edifice, with its lowly roof of thatch, where, for eight years of sadness, Wilson and Cotton, with their exiled flock, worshiped in spirit and in truth the Father who "seeketh such to worship him." Let that humble structure be commemorated with those wattled temples, in which the first converts to Christianity among our British sires, who dwelt in what was then a land as savage and heathen as was this, before the pilgrims came, sang high praises to the babe that was laid in the manger at Bethlehem.

The second house of worship was built in what is now called Cornhill Square in 1640. After standing for seventy-one years, it was rebuilt in Cornhill Square in 1712. After the lapse of near a century, the First Church removed, and built the present meeting-house in Chauncy Place. Oh, who that passes by that venerated sanctuary, can refrain from calling to mind that holy and apostolic succession of men of God, from the warm-hearted Wilson to the orthodox and eloquent Foxcroft, who have ministered to that famous Church, and the multitude of its sainted dead? And who that reflects upon the fearful falling away of that assembly from the faith of their fathers, can suppress the lamentation of the prophet, "How is the gold become dim! how is the most fine gold changed!"[36]

Baptisms

During the nineteen years and more that Mr. Cotton presided in that Church, one thousand and thirty-four children received the seal of baptism. Of these four hundred and fifty-six were females, and five hundred and thirty-eight were males, being a large excess in favor of the latter. The number of baptisms in each year, exceeded fifty. On this duty of sealing the children of the covenant, and placing Christ's mark upon the lambs of his flock, the teacher laid great stress, and imparted much instruction, some part of which remains in print.

Admissions to the Church

During the same period, there were admitted to the Church three hundred and six men, and three hundred and forty-three women: in all six hundred and forty-nine, being an average of thirty-four admissions in each year.

---

[36] Lamentations 4:1.

Seventeen persons had been publicly admonished for different offenses; and five of them who could not be reclaimed were cut off by excommunication. Considering the numbers of the Church, and the strictness of the watch and discipline then maintained, so small a number of ecclesiastical censures argues great purity and blamelessness on the part of the members at large.

Children & Grandchildren

Mr. Cotton had three sons and as many daughters, all by his second wife. Seaborn Cotton, his oldest child, graduated at Harvard College in 1651. He was ordained the second minister of Hampton in New Hampshire in 1660, where he spent his days in great usefulness and honor. He died the nineteenth of April, 1686, aged fifty-two years. He was succeeded by his own son, John Cotton, who also died there at the same age of fifty-two.

The second son of the patriarch of Boston, John Cotton the younger, graduated at Harvard College in 1657. For several years he preached to the Indians at Martha's Vineyard in their own language. He was ordained at Plymouth in 1669, and labored there in the ministry with great diligence and success for thirty years, both among the whites and Indians. In his fifty-ninth year he removed to Charleston, South Carolina, where he gathered the Congregational Church, which still exists, and is one of the principal churches in that city. He died in less than a year after, on the eighteenth of September, 1669. His son, Roland Cotton, graduated at Harvard in 1680, and was ordained the first minister of Sandwich, Massachusetts, in 1694. He also preached to the Marshpee Indians, of whom, in 1693, two hundred and fourteen were under his care, while five hundred others in the neighborhood of Plymouth were under the care of his father. Roland Cotton died at Sandwich in 1722. He had a brother, Josiah Cotton, who graduated at Harvard in 1698. He was Clerk of Court, Register of Deeds, and Judge of the Common Pleas. He also preached to the Indians at five different stations for nearly forty years. He died the nineteenth of August, 1756, aged seventy-five. Three other brothers of Roland and Josiah were ministers. Roland had three sons who were ministers of repute, John Cotton at Newton, Nathaniel Cotton of Bristol, and Ward Cotton of Boylston. Josiah Cotton of Plymouth had a son John, who was the first minister of Halifax.

There have been many other descendants of the Boston minister, who have inherited his name and calling. In him there was a fulfillment of the promise, "My Spirit that is upon thee, and my words which I have put in thy mouth, shall not depart out of thy mouth, nor out of the mouth of thy seed, nor out of the mouth of thy seed's seed, saith the Lord, from henceforth and forever." [37] It may be said of the posterity of very many of the pious settlers of this "New English Canaan" — "Their seed shall be known among the Gentiles, and their offspring among

---

[37] Isaiah 59:20–21.

the people: all that see them shall acknowledge them, that they are the seed which the Lord hath blessed."[38]

But we must revert to the immediate family of the venerable saint of Boston. His youngest son, Roland, and his oldest daughter, Sarah, died nearly at the same time, at an early age, of the small pox, which raged in Boston in 1649. Sarah died on the twentieth of November. Her last words to her parents were, "Pray, my dear father, let me now go home." In a few lines of his we find the following language of pious acquiescence in this affecting wish—

> Go then, sweet Sara, take thy Sabbath rest,
> With thy great Lord, and all in heaven, blest.[39]

Roland died nine days after his sister, on which sad occasion, the submissive father again vented his feelings in his antiquated measures:

> Suffer, saith Christ, your little ones,
>   To come forth, me unto,
> For of such ones my kingdom is.
>   Of grace and glory too.
> We do not only *suffer* them,
>   But *offer* them to thee;
> Now, blessed Lord, let us believe,
>   Accepted that they be.[40]

---

[38] Isaiah 61:9
[39] Mather, *Magnalia*, 260.
[40] Mather, *Magnalia*, 260.

Of Mr. Cotton's younger daughters, one was married to a respectable merchant by the name of Egginton, but did not long survive the birth of her only child. The child also in a few years followed the mother to the grave. The other daughter of Mr. Cotton became the wife of Increase Mather, D. D., one of the most useful men to Massachusetts whom that "mother of great men" has ever produced. Through Mrs. Mather, her father became the ancestor of several of the most distinguished ministers of the country. His celebrated grandson, Cotton Mather, in our days so grossly slandered and maligned, has noticed an interesting fact in regard to the second, or Old North Church in Boston. The formation of this church, in 1649, appeared to be quite detrimental to the interests of Mr. Cotton, and yet he cheerfully encouraged the undertaking, because it seemed to be required by the interests of religion. Now, of that very church, his son-in-law was pastor above threescore years, and his grandson for forty-four.

Mr. Cotton's Widow

Mr. Cotton's widow became the second wife of Rev. Richard Mather of Dorchester, the father of her son-in-law, to whom she thus became a parent by a double affinity. She survived her second husband, with whom she lived in great happiness for many years.

Woodbridge's Elegy

We thus close our account of John Cotton, and those connected with him. That star rose brightly on the older England, and rode through stormy skies. But it sweetly shed its parting rays on the newer England, at its serene and unclouded setting. We close with the following extract from his funeral elegy, by Benjamin Woodbridge, D.D., which, doubtless, afforded to the philosophic printer, Dr. Franklin, the hint of his famous epitaph upon himself—

> A living, breathing Bible; tables where
>   Best covenants at large engraven were;
> Gospel and law in his heart had each its column;
>   His head an index to the sacred volume;
> His very name a title-page; and next
>   His life a commentary on the text.
> O what a monument of glorious worth,
>   When in a new edition he comes forth
> Without erratas, may we think he'll be.
>   In leaves and covers of eternity.[41]

---

[41] Mather, *Magnalia*, 284.

Works Cited

While the author cites from various sources, the following constitutes his primary sources of research:

William Ives Budington, *History of the First Church in Charlestown*. Boston: C. Tappan, 1845.

William Hubbard, *A General History of New England*. Boston: Charles C. Little and James Brown, 1848.

Thomas Hutchinson, *The History of the Province of Massachusetts-Bay*, vol. 1. Boston: Thomas and John Fleet, 1828.

Cotton Mather, *Magnalia Christi Americana*. London: Thomas Parkhurst, 1702.

John Norton, *Memoir of John Cotton*. Enoch Pond, ed. Boston: Perkins & Marvin, 1834.

John Winthrop, *The History of New England from 1630 to 1649*, vol. 1. James Savage, ed. Boston: Little, Brown and Company, 1853.

The Writings of John Cotton

As recorded in the 1834 edition of John Norton's *Memoir of John Cotton*.

God's Promise to his Plantation: An Election Sermon, in 1634.

A Letter in Answer to Objections made against the New England Churches; with the Questions proposed to such as are admitted to church fellowship. 1641.

The Way of Life. 4to.

God's mercy mixed with Justice.

An Abstract of the Laws of New England. 1641. (This abstract of such laws of the Jews as were supposed to be of perpetual obligation was drawn up in 1636. It is preserved in Vol. 5th of the Mass. Historical Collections.)

The Church's Resurrection; on the fifth and sixth verses of the 20th chapter of Revelation.

An Answer to Mr. Ball's Discourse on set Forms of Prayer.

Exposition of Revelation, xvi.

The true Constitution of a Particular, Visible Church. 1643.

The Keys of the Kingdom of Heaven, and power thereof. 1644.

The Doctrine of the Church, to which is committed the Keys of the Kingdom of Heaven.

The Covenant of God's Free Grace most sweetly unfolded. 1645.

The Way of the Churches of Christ in New England.

The Pouring out of the Seven Vials.

The Controversy concerning Liberty of Conscience truly stated. 1646.

The Singing of Psalms a Gospel Ordinance. 1647.

The Grounds and Ends of the Baptism of Children. 1647.

A Letter to Mr. Roger Williams.

The Bloody Tenet washed and made white in the Blood of the Lamb; in Answer to Mr. Williams.

Questions propounded in Mr. Cotton by the Teaching Elders, with his Answers to each Question.

The Way of Congregational Churches cleared, in two Treatises, against Mr. Baylie and Mr. Rutherford. 1648.

The Holiness of Church Members, proving that Visible Saints are the matter of the Church. 1650.

Christ the Fountain of Life. 1651.

A brief Exposition of Ecclesiastes. 1652.

A Censure upon the Way of Mr. Henden of Kent.

Sermons on the first Epistle of John. Folio.

A Discourse on things indifferent; proving that no church Governors have power to impose indifferent things upon the Conscience of Men.

Exposition of Canticles.

Milk for Babes: a Catechism.

Meat for Strong Men.

A Discourse about Civil Government in a Plantation whose design in religion.

Date Completed	Name

H&E *Publishing*

WWW.HESEDANDEMET.COM

www.ingramcontent.com/pod-product-compliance
Lightning Source LLC
Chambersburg PA
CBHW020533080526

44583CB00013B/843